Best of Country
Chicken

Chicken Makes
a Good Dinner Great!

ADD VARIETY to your menu with any of the 197 recipes shared in the *Best of Country Chicken*. Versatile and economical, chicken is always a welcome addition to a dinner table. In addition to many family favorites, you'll also find a selection of new and different ways to prepare this time-tested poultry.

But, before you get started, turn to the Chicken Reference Guide on pages 4 and 5. Many recipes, such as Pineapple Pepper Chicken on page 5, call for a broiler/fryer chicken cut up. The step-by-step photos show you how! Or when you want to carve up a tasty bird, refer to page 4 for some tips you can use for chicken or turkey.

From tasty kabobs to traditional roasted chicken, this book features recipes from some of the best cooks in the country. We searched our files to compile the *Best of Country Chicken*. With 197 recipes, this book is chock-full of treasured recipes from past issues of *Taste of Home* and its "sister" publications.

You can make these recipes with confidence because each and every one is a tried-and-true favorite of a fellow cook's family. Our test kitchen staff prepared and taste-tasted each recipe, helping to make this a book we can call "The Best." But we'll let you decide which recipes will become your *Best of Country Chicken!*

Editor: Beth Wittlinger
Art Director: Maribeth Greinke
Executive Editor, Books: Heidi Reuter Lloyd
Associate Editor: Jean Steiner
Proofreader: Julie Blume
Graphic Art Associates: Ellen Lloyd, Catherine Fletcher
Editorial Assistant: Barb Czysz
Food Editor: Janaan Cunningham
Associate Food Editors: Coleen Martin, Diane Werner
Senior Recipe Editor: Sue A. Jurack
Recipe Editor: Jan Briggs
Food Photographers: Rob Hagen, Dan Roberts, Jim Wieland
Set Stylists: Julie Ferron, Stephanie Marchese, Sue Myers, Jennifer Bradley Vent
Food Stylists: Kristin Arnett, Sarah Thompson, Joylyn Trickel
Photographers Assistant: Lori Foy

Senior Vice President, Editor in Chief: Catherine Cassidy
President: Barbara Newton
Chairman and Founder: Roy Reiman

©2005 Reiman Media Group, Inc.
5400 S. 60th St., Greendale WI 53129
International Standard Book Number: 0-89821-454-8
Library of Congress Control Number: 2005929260
All rights reserved.
Printed in U.S.A.

Pictured on front cover: Thyme Herbed Chicken (p. 4).
Pictured on back cover: Sunday Fried Chicken (p. 88) and feather photo from Maslowski Productions.

Best of Country Chicken

Makes a Great Gift!

To order additional copies of the *Best of Country Chicken* book, specify item number 35292 and send $15.99 (plus $4.95 shipping/insured delivery for one book, $5.50 for two or more) to: Country Store, Suite 7900, P.O. Box 990, Greendale WI 53129-0990. To order by credit card, call toll-free 1-800/558-1013 or visit our Web site at *www.reimanpub.com*.

Chicken
Reference Guide

While trying out some of the recipes in the *Best of Country Chicken*, you may find many that call for a whole broiler/fryer chicken or a cut-up broiler/fryer chicken. Below is a recipe for a roasted chicken followed by a handy guide to carving. On page 5, you will see easy-to-follow photos that show you how to cut up a whole chicken and use it in a recipe. For other recipes using whole broiler/fryer chickens, refer to the Index on page 109.

Thyme Herbed Chicken

(Pictured at left and on the cover)

Polly Lloyd, Burlington, Wisconsin

My family and friends always comment on the wonderful herb flavors in this chicken recipe. The herbs make great seasoning for the vegetables, too!

```
3/4 to 1 cup water
   1 tablespoon chicken bouillon granules
 3/4 teaspoon dried thyme
 1/2 teaspoon dried marjoram
 1/4 teaspoon lemon-pepper seasoning
   1 broiler/fryer chicken (3-1/2 to 4 pounds)
   1 pound red potatoes, halved
   2 medium onions, cut into 1/2-inch pieces
1-1/2 to 2 cups fresh baby carrots
```

Combine the water, bouillon, thyme, marjoram and lemon-pepper; pour into a roasting pan. Add chicken; arrange potatoes, onions and carrots around it.

Cover and bake at 350° for 50 minutes. Uncover; bake for 20-30 minutes or until vegetables are tender and chicken juices run clear. **Yield:** 4 servings.

Carving Basics

1 Pull leg away from body and cut between the thigh joint and the body to remove entire leg. Repeat with other leg. Disjoint drumstick and thigh. Hold each part by the bone and cut off 1/4-in. slices.

2 Hold the bird with a meat fork and make a deep cut into the breast meat just above the wing area.

3 Slice down from the top of the breast into the cut made in Step 2. Slice meat 1/4 in. thick.

Pineapple Pepper Chicken

(Pictured above)

Phyllis Minter, Wakefield, Kansas

I came up with this recipe years ago by combining a couple of family favorites. Easy and versatile, it's great for potlucks. I can make the sauce ahead and use all wings or leg quarters when they're on sale. This is a welcome entree at senior citizen fellowship dinners.

> 4 cups unsweetened pineapple juice
> 2-1/2 cups sugar
> 2 cups vinegar
> 1-1/2 cups water
> 1 cup packed brown sugar
> 2/3 cup cornstarch
> 1/2 cup ketchup
> 6 tablespoons soy sauce
> 2 teaspoons chicken bouillon granules
> 3/4 teaspoon ground ginger
> 3 tablespoons vegetable oil
> 2 broiler/fryer chickens (3 to 3-1/2 pounds *each*), cut up
> 1 can (8 ounces) pineapple chunks, drained
> 1 medium green pepper, julienned

In a saucepan, combine the first 10 ingredients; stir until smooth. Bring to a boil; cook and stir for 2 minutes or until thickened. Set aside. Heat oil in a large skillet over medium-high heat. Add the chicken; brown on all sides.

Place in two greased 13-in. x 9-in. x 2-in. baking dishes. Pour reserved sauce over chicken. Bake, uncovered, at 350° for 45 minutes. Add pineapple and green pepper. Bake 15 minutes longer or until heated through. **Yield:** 12 servings.

Cutting Up a Whole Chicken

1 Pull leg and thigh away from body. With a small sharp knife, cut through the skin to expose the joint.

2 Cut through joint, then cut the skin around the drumstick to free the leg. Repeat with the other leg.

3 To separate the drumstick from the thigh, cut the skin at joint. Bend drumstick to expose the joint; cut through the joint and skin.

4 Pull the wing away from the body. Cut through skin to expose joint. Cut through joint and skin to separate the wing from the body. Repeat with other wing.

5 With a kitchen or poultry shears, snip along each side of the backbone between rib joints.

6 Hold chicken breast in both hands (skin side down) and bend it back to snap breastbone. Turn over. With a knife, cut in half along breastbone. The breastbone will remain attached to one of the halves.

6

1 Soups, Salads & Sandwiches

Chicken Tortellini Soup

(Pictured at left)

Jean Atherly, Red Lodge, Montana

I love experimenting with recipes and mixing ingredients to come up with original dishes. This soup is great with a simple salad and breadsticks.

    2 cans (14-1/2 ounces *each*) chicken broth
    2 cups water
1-1/2 cups frozen mixed vegetables
    3 boneless skinless chicken breast halves, cut
      into 1-inch cubes
    1 package (8 to 9 ounces) refrigerated cheese
      tortellini
    2 celery ribs, thinly sliced
    1 teaspoon dried basil
  1/2 teaspoon dried oregano
  1/2 teaspoon garlic salt
  1/4 teaspoon pepper
Breadsticks, optional

In a 3-qt. saucepan, combine the first 10 ingredients; bring to a boil. Reduce heat; cover and simmer for 20 minutes. Serve with breadsticks if desired. **Yield:** 8 servings (about 2 quarts).

Sesame Chicken Over Greens

Diana Mullins, Lexington, Kentucky

The grilled chicken strips make this salad hearty enough for a meal…but the assorted fresh veggies keep it nice and light. My sons can't get enough of it!

✓ Uses less fat, sugar or salt. Includes Nutritional Analysis and Diabetic Exchanges.

  1/4 cup reduced-sodium teriyaki sauce
    2 tablespoons red wine vinegar
    2 tablespoons canola oil
    2 tablespoons honey
    2 teaspoons crushed red pepper flakes
    1 garlic clove, minced
    4 boneless skinless chicken breast halves
      (1 pound)
    5 cups torn mixed salad greens
  1/2 cup sliced sweet red pepper
  1/2 cup shredded carrot
    4 green onions, sliced
    1 can (2-1/4 ounces) sliced ripe olives, drained
  1/2 cup reduced-fat ranch salad dressing
    1 tablespoon sesame seeds, toasted

In a large resealable plastic bag, combine the first six ingredients; mix well. Add chicken; seal bag and turn to coat. Refrigerate for several hours or overnight.

Drain and discard marinade. Grill chicken, uncovered, over medium heat for 5-7 minutes on each side or until juices run clear.

On four serving plates, divide the greens, red pepper, carrot, onions and olives. Thinly slice chicken and arrange over salad. Drizzle with ranch dressing; sprinkle with sesame seeds. **Yield:** 4 servings.

Nutritional Analysis: One serving (1 chicken breast half with about 1-1/2 cups salad and 2 tablespoons dressing) equals 347 calories, 16 g fat (2 g saturated fat), 71 mg cholesterol, 788 mg sodium, 21 g carbohydrate, 2 g fiber, 30 g protein. **Diabetic Exchanges:** 3-1/2 lean meat, 2 fat, 2 vegetable.

Curried Chicken Tea Sandwiches

Robin Fuhrman, Fond du Lac, Wisconsin

At the Victorian-theme bridal shower I hosted, I spread this dressed-up chicken salad on heart-shaped bread.

    2 cups cubed cooked chicken
    1 medium unpeeled red apple, chopped
  3/4 cup dried cranberries
  1/2 cup thinly sliced celery
  1/4 cup chopped pecans
    2 tablespoons thinly sliced green onions
  3/4 cup mayonnaise
    2 teaspoons lime juice
  1/2 to 3/4 teaspoon curry powder
   12 slices bread
Lettuce leaves

In a bowl, combine the first six ingredients. In another bowl, combine the mayonnaise, lime juice and curry powder; add to chicken mixture and stir to coat. Cover and refrigerate until serving.

Cut each slice of bread with a 3-in. heart-shaped cookie cutter if desired. Top with lettuce and chicken salad. **Yield:** 6 servings.

Fruity Chicken Pasta Salad

Roberta Freedman, Mesilla Park, New Mexico

I use this recipe whenever we go to a potluck dinner. It always gets rave reviews because of its great mixture of flavors. It's a nice way to use up leftover chicken.

  8 ounces uncooked spiral pasta
  1 can (20 ounces) pineapple chunks
  3 to 4 cups cubed cooked chicken
  1 can (15-1/2 ounces) sliced peaches, drained and diced
  2 tablespoons raisins
1/3 cup vegetable oil
1/4 cup soy sauce
  1 teaspoon curry powder
1/2 cup chopped pecans

Cook pasta according to package directions; rinse with cold water and drain. Drain pineapple, reserving 1/2 cup juice. Dice the pineapple and place in a large bowl. Add pasta, chicken, peaches and raisins.

In a small bowl, whisk together oil, soy sauce, curry powder and reserved pineapple juice. Pour over pasta mixture; toss to coat. Cover and refrigerate for 2 hours. Stir in pecans just before serving. **Yield:** 6-8 servings.

Chicken Wild Rice Soup

(Pictured above)

Virginia Montmarquet, Riverside, California

I'm originally from Minnesota, where wild rice grows in abundance. This soup has been part of my family's menu for years. To save time, I cook the chicken and wild rice and cut up the vegetables the day before.

  2 quarts chicken broth
1/2 pound fresh mushrooms, chopped
  1 cup finely chopped celery
  1 cup shredded carrots
1/2 cup finely chopped onion
  1 teaspoon chicken bouillon granules
  1 teaspoon dried parsley flakes
1/4 teaspoon garlic powder
1/4 teaspoon dried thyme
1/4 cup butter
1/4 cup all-purpose flour
  1 can (10-3/4 ounces) condensed cream of mushroom soup, undiluted
1/2 cup dry white wine *or* additional chicken broth
  3 cups cooked wild rice
  2 cups cubed cooked chicken

In a large saucepan, combine the first nine ingredients. Bring to a boil. Reduce heat; cover and simmer for 30 minutes.

In a Dutch oven or soup kettle, melt butter. Stir in flour until smooth. Gradually whisk in broth mixture. Bring to a boil; cook and stir for 2 minutes or until thickened. Whisk in soup and wine or broth. Add rice and chicken; heat through. **Yield:** 14 servings (3-1/2 quarts).

Caesar Chicken Potato Salad

(Pictured below)

Sarita Johnston, San Antonio, Texas

Here in Texas, we seem to have summer year-round. So quick-to-fix dishes like this that get you in and out of the kitchen are popular.

4 cups quartered small white *or* red potatoes
3/4 pound boneless skinless chicken breasts, cubed
1 tablespoon vegetable oil
1 package (10 ounces) mixed salad greens
1 small red onion, sliced and separated into rings
3/4 cup Caesar salad dressing
1/3 cup croutons
2 tablespoons shredded Parmesan cheese

Place potatoes in a large saucepan and cover with water. Cover and bring to a boil over medium-high heat; cook for 15-20 minutes or until tender.

Meanwhile, in a skillet, saute chicken in oil for 5-10 minutes or until juices run clear. Drain potatoes; add to chicken.

Place greens and onion in a serving bowl. Top with chicken mixture. Drizzle with dressing; sprinkle with the croutons and cheese. Serve immediately. **Yield:** 4 servings.

Buffalo Chicken Calzones

Ruth Ann Riendeau
Twin Mountain, New Hampshire

I'm always looking to jazz up pizza. This recipe also incorporates my love of buffalo chicken wings.

1 can (8 ounces) pizza sauce
2 teaspoons plus 1/2 cup hot pepper sauce, *divided*
1-1/4 pounds boneless skinless chicken breasts, cubed
3 celery ribs, chopped
3 tablespoons butter
Dash Cajun seasoning
2 tubes (10 ounces *each*) refrigerated pizza crust dough
1-1/2 cups (6 ounces) shredded Monterey Jack cheese
4 ounces crumbled blue cheese
Cornmeal

In a bowl, combine pizza sauce and 2 teaspoons hot pepper sauce; set aside. In a skillet, saute chicken and celery in butter for 3-5 minutes or until chicken is no longer pink. Stir in Cajun seasoning and the remaining hot pepper sauce; cover and simmer for 10-15 minutes or until heated through.

Unroll pizza dough; divide each portion in half. On a floured surface, roll each into an 8-in. circle. Spread pizza sauce mixture over half of each circle to within 1 in. of edges. Top with chicken mixture and cheeses. Fold dough over filling; pinch edges to seal.

Sprinkle greased baking sheets with cornmeal. Place calzones over cornmeal. Bake at 400° for 10-12 minutes or until golden brown. **Yield:** 4 calzones.

Warm Apricot Chicken Salad

(Pictured above)

Carolyn Popwell, Lacey, Washington

Fresh apricots star in this delightful salad, which is topped with marinated chicken. Even our kids like the sweet and tangy flavor.

✓ Uses less fat, sugar or salt. Includes Nutritional Analysis and Diabetic Exchanges.

1 pound boneless skinless chicken breasts, cut into strips
2 tablespoons orange marmalade fruit spread
1 tablespoon reduced-sodium soy sauce
6 fresh apricots, sliced
2 teaspoons grated orange peel
1/2 pound fresh spinach, stems removed
1 medium sweet red pepper, julienned
1 tablespoon vegetable oil
1/4 cup fat-free ranch salad dressing
1/4 cup slivered almonds, toasted

In a large bowl, combine chicken, marmalade and soy sauce. Cover and refrigerate for 20-30 minutes. Meanwhile, toss apricots and orange peel. Place spinach on a serving platter or four salad plates; top with apricots.

In a skillet, saute red pepper and chicken mixture in oil until chicken juices run clear. Remove from the heat; stir in salad dressing. Spoon over spinach and apricots; sprinkle with almonds. **Yield:** 4 servings.

Nutritional Analysis: One serving equals 303 calories, 388 g sodium, 63 mg cholesterol, 24 g carbohydrate, 28 g protein, 11 g fat, 3 g fiber. **Diabetic Exchanges:** 3-1/2 meat, 1 vegetable, 1 fruit.

Bake, uncovered, at 400° for 12 minutes. Turn chicken. Bake 8-12 minutes longer or until juices run clear and coating is lightly browned. Serve on rolls with lettuce and tomato. **Yield:** 6 servings.

Nutritional Analysis: One sandwich equals 372 calories, 7 g fat (3 g saturated fat), 63 mg cholesterol, 759 mg sodium, 46 g carbohydrate, 3 g fiber, 31 g protein. **Diabetic Exchanges:** 3 lean meat, 3 starch.

Curried Chicken Pockets

Lisa Scandrette, Eveleth, Minnesota

I served these pitas stuffed with zippy chicken filling for a picnic the day my husband and I got engaged. Now our children enjoy them.

  1/2 **cup mayonnaise**
  1/2 **cup chutney**
    1 **tablespoon curry powder**
    6 **cups cubed cooked chicken**
PITA BREAD:
    1 **package (1/4 ounce) active dry yeast**
1-1/3 **cups warm water (110° to 115°),** *divided*
    3 **to 3-1/2 cups all-purpose flour**
    1 **tablespoon vegetable oil**
    1 **teaspoon salt**
  1/4 **teaspoon sugar**
    3 **tablespoons cornmeal**
Lettuce leaves

In a bowl, combine the mayonnaise, chutney, curry powder and chicken; refrigerate until serving.

In a mixing bowl, dissolve yeast in 1/3 cup warm water. Add 1-1/2 cups of flour, oil, salt, sugar and remaining water; beat until smooth. Add enough remaining flour to form a soft dough. Turn onto a floured surface; knead until smooth and elastic, about 10 minutes. Place in a greased bowl, turning once to grease top. Cover and let rise in a warm place until doubled, about 1 hour. Punch dough down; shape into six balls. Let rise for 30 minutes.

Sprinkle three ungreased baking sheets with cornmeal. Roll each ball into a 7-in. circle. Place two circles on each baking sheet. Let rise for 30 minutes. Bake at 500° for 10 minutes or until lightly browned. Cool. Cut pitas in half. Line each with lettuce; fill with 1/3 cup chicken mixture. **Yield:** 12 sandwiches.

Ultimate Chicken Sandwiches

(Pictured above)

Greg Voss, Emerson, Nebraska

After making these sandwiches, you'll never order the fast-food kind again. Marinating the chicken in buttermilk gives it a wonderful taste.

✓ Uses less fat, sugar or salt. Includes Nutritional Analysis and Diabetic Exchanges.

    6 **boneless skinless chicken breast halves**
      (4 ounces *each***)**
    1 **cup 1% buttermilk**
  1/2 **cup reduced-fat biscuit/baking mix**
  1/2 **cup cornmeal**
1-1/2 **teaspoons paprika**
  3/4 **teaspoon salt**
  3/4 **teaspoon poultry seasoning**
  1/2 **teaspoon garlic powder**
  1/2 **teaspoon pepper**
  1/4 **teaspoon cayenne pepper**
    6 **onion** *or* **kaiser rolls, split**
    6 **lettuce leaves**
  12 **tomato slices**

Pound chicken to 1/2-in. thickness. Pour buttermilk into a large resealable plastic bag; add chicken. Seal bag and turn to coat; refrigerate for 8 hours or overnight.

In a shallow bowl, combine the biscuit mix, cornmeal, paprika, salt, poultry seasoning, garlic powder, pepper and cayenne. Remove chicken one piece at a time, allowing excess buttermilk to drain off. Discard buttermilk.

Coat chicken with the cornmeal mixture; place in a 13-in. x 9-in. x 2-in. baking dish coated with nonstick cooking spray.

The Trick to Buttermilk

For extra-crispy chicken, dip it in buttermilk before coating with all-purpose flour. Buttermilk will hold more flour on the chicken for a thicker coating.

"Bring an Ingredient" Soup

(Pictured below)

Mary Anne McWhirter, Pearland, Texas

A steaming bowl of soup packed with vegetables and meat is just the thing to take the chill off a cold winter evening. Asking each guest to bring an ingredient adds to the fun of a potluck or gathering. But, best of all, it means less fuss for you!

4 cups thinly sliced onions
1 garlic clove, minced
3 tablespoons butter
3 tablespoons all-purpose flour
6 cans (14-1/2 ounces *each*) beef broth
2 cups tomato puree
1 tablespoon red wine vinegar
1 tablespoon Worcestershire sauce
1 tablespoon sugar
1/2 teaspoon *each* dried oregano, tarragon, ground cumin, salt and pepper
1/4 to 1/2 teaspoon hot pepper sauce

VEGETABLES (choose two or three):
1-1/2 cups *each* diced green pepper, tomato *or* carrots
2 cups sliced fresh mushrooms
MEATS (choose two):
3 cups cooked mini meatballs
3 cups cubed cooked chicken
3 cups diced fully cooked ham
1 package (10 ounces) smoked kielbasa, sliced and browned
GARNISHES (choose three or four):
Shredded cheddar cheese, garbanzo beans, sour cream, chopped fresh parsley, croutons *or* popcorn

In a large Dutch oven, saute the onions and garlic in butter until tender. Stir in flour and blend well. Add broth, puree, vinegar, Worcestershire sauce, sugar and seasonings; mix well. Bring to a boil; reduce heat and simmer for 40 minutes.

Add vegetables; simmer for 30 minutes or until tender. Add meats; heat through. Garnish as desired. **Yield:** 16-18 servings (4-1/2 quarts).

Chicken Fajita Salad

(Pictured below)

Audrey Thibodeau, Mesa, Arizona

Living in the Southwest, I've learned to create all sorts of Mexican dishes. This nicely spiced salad is one of my favorites. It's a winner with my luncheon guests.

      6 tablespoons vegetable oil, *divided*
  1/2 cup lime juice
      2 tablespoons minced fresh parsley
      2 garlic cloves, minced
      1 teaspoon ground cumin
      1 teaspoon dried oregano
1-1/4 pounds boneless skinless chicken
        breasts, cut into 1-inch pieces
      1 cup sliced green onions
      1 medium sweet red pepper, julienned
      1 can (4 ounces) chopped green chilies,
        drained
      1 cup chopped pecans, toasted
Shredded lettuce
      2 medium tomatoes, cut into wedges
      1 medium ripe avocado, peeled and sliced
Tortillas, warmed, optional

In a bowl, combine 4 tablespoons oil, lime juice, parsley, garlic, cumin and oregano. Pour half into a large resealable plastic bag; add the chicken. Seal bag and turn to coat; refrigerate for 1 hour or overnight. Cover and refrigerate remaining marinade. Drain and discard marinade from chicken.

In a large skillet, saute onions in remaining oil for 2 minutes. Add chicken; stir-fry for 2-3 minutes or until

chicken just begins to brown and juices run clear. Add the red pepper, chilies and reserved marinade; stir-fry for 2 minutes. Stir in pecans.

Place lettuce on individual plates; top with chicken mixture, tomatoes and avocado. Serve with tortillas if desired. **Yield:** 4 servings.

Red, White and Blue Chili

(Pictured above)

Dotty Parker, Christmas Valley, Oregon

Instead of the usual picnic fare, I surprised family and guests with this mild-flavored dish one Independence Day. They were delighted with the colorful chips and chili.

      1 medium green pepper, diced
  1/4 cup diced onion
      2 garlic cloves, minced
      1 tablespoon vegetable oil
      2 cans (14-1/2 ounces *each*) Mexican diced
        tomatoes, undrained
      2 cans (14-1/2 ounces *each*) chicken broth
      2 cups shredded cooked chicken
      2 cans (15-1/2 ounces *each*) great
        northern beans, rinsed and drained
      1 can (16 ounces) kidney beans, rinsed and
        drained

1 envelope chili seasoning
1 tablespoon brown sugar
1 teaspoon salt
1/4 teaspoon pepper
Blue tortilla chips

In a Dutch oven or soup kettle, saute the green pepper, onion and garlic in oil until tender. Stir in the tomatoes, broth, chicken, beans, chili seasoning, brown sugar, salt and pepper.

Bring to a boil. Reduce heat; cover and simmer for 45 minutes. Serve with tortilla chips. **Yield:** 8 servings (about 2 quarts).

Orange-Avocado Chicken Salad

Shelia Garcia, Mantachie, Mississippi

Orange sections and avocado slices surround this hearty salad, making for a pretty presentation. It's a refreshing summer main dish for both lunch and dinner.

1/4 cup lime juice
2 teaspoons salt, *divided*
4 cups cubed cooked chicken
2 cups frozen peas, thawed
1 cup coarsely chopped carrots
1/2 cup thinly sliced celery
1/3 cup minced fresh parsley
1 cup mayonnaise
3 tablespoons orange juice
1/4 teaspoon pepper
Torn salad greens
6 medium navel oranges, peeled and sectioned
4 medium ripe avocados, peeled and sliced
1/4 cup thinly sliced green onions

In a small bowl, combine lime juice and 3/4 teaspoon salt; cover and refrigerate. In a large bowl, combine the chicken, peas, carrots, celery and parsley. Combine the mayonnaise, orange juice, pepper and remaining salt; pour over chicken mixture and toss to coat. Cover and refrigerate for at least 1 hour.

Place greens on a serving platter or individual plates. Top with chicken salad; arrange orange sections and avocado slices around salad. Sprinkle with green onions. Drizzle with lime juice mixture. **Yield:** 12 servings.

Lime Appeal

Limes store best at 40-45° F and last only about 2 weeks. It takes about 10 limes to yield about 1 cup of juice.

Sizzling Rice Soup

(Pictured below)

Mary Woodke, Gardiner, New York

My family enjoys food with flair like this unique soup. Whenever I serve it, it's such a hit that no one has much room for the main course. The children get a real kick out of watching the rice sizzle when it gets added to the soup.

1 cup uncooked long grain rice
8 cups chicken broth
2 cups cubed cooked chicken
2 cups sliced fresh mushrooms
1/4 cup chopped green onions
1 can (8 ounces) bamboo shoots, drained
1 can (8 ounces) sliced water chestnuts, drained
4 chicken bouillon cubes
1/2 teaspoon garlic powder
1 package (10 ounces) frozen peas
1/4 cup vegetable oil

Cook rice according to package directions. Spread on a greased 15-in. x 10-in. x 1-in. baking pan. Bake at 325° for 2 hours or until dried and browned, stirring occasionally; set aside.

In a large soup kettle or Dutch oven, combine the broth, chicken, mushrooms, onions, bamboo shoots, water chestnuts, bouillon and garlic powder. Cover and simmer for 1 hour. Add peas; cook for 15 minutes.

Just before serving, heat oil in a skillet. Fry rice in hot oil until it is slightly puffed. Ladle soup into serving bowls. Immediately spoon some hot rice into each bowl and it will sizzle. **Yield:** 10-12 servings (3 quarts).

Baked Deli Sandwich

(Pictured above)

Sandra McKenzie, Braham, Minnesota

Frozen bread dough and quick baking time make this stuffed sandwich one I rely on often.

- 1 loaf (1 pound) frozen bread dough, thawed
- 2 tablespoons butter, melted
- 1/4 teaspoon garlic salt
- 1/4 teaspoon dried basil
- 1/4 teaspoon dried oregano
- 1/4 teaspoon pizza seasoning
- 1/4 pound sliced deli ham
- 6 thin slices mozzarella cheese
- 1/4 pound sliced deli smoked chicken *or* turkey breast
- 6 thin slices cheddar cheese

Pizza sauce, warmed, optional

On a baking sheet coated with nonstick cooking spray, roll dough into a small rectangle. Let rest for 5-10 minutes. In a small bowl, combine the butter and seasonings. Roll out dough into a 14-in. x 10-in. rectangle. Brush with half of the butter mixture.

Layer the ham, mozzarella cheese, chicken and cheddar cheese lengthwise over half of the dough to within 1/2 in. of edges. Fold dough over and pinch firmly to seal. Brush with remaining butter mixture.

Bake at 400° for 10-12 minutes or until golden brown. Cut into 1-in. slices. Serve immediately with pizza sauce if desired. **Yield:** 4-6 servings.

Cream of Wild Rice Soup

J. Beatrice Hintz, Neenah, Wisconsin

Tender cubes of chicken, fresh vegetables and wild rice make this soup hearty enough for a meal. You can't beat the down-home comfort of a warm bowlful.

 Uses less fat, sugar or salt. Includes Nutritional Analysis and Diabetic Exchanges.

- 1 large onion, chopped
- 1 large carrot, shredded
- 1 celery rib, chopped
- 1/4 cup butter
- 1/2 cup all-purpose flour
- 8 cups chicken broth
- 3 cups cooked wild rice

1 cup cubed cooked chicken breast
1/4 teaspoon salt
1/4 teaspoon pepper
1 cup fat-free evaporated milk
1/4 cup snipped chives

In a large saucepan, saute the onion, carrot and celery in butter until tender. Stir in flour until blended. Gradually add broth. Stir in the rice, chicken, salt and pepper. Bring to a boil over medium heat; cook and stir for 2 minutes or until thickened. Stir in milk; cook 3-5 minutes longer. Garnish with chives. **Yield:** 10 servings (2-1/2 quarts).

   Nutritional Analysis: One serving (1 cup) equals 180 calories, 6 g fat (3 g saturated fat), 25 mg cholesterol, 899 mg sodium, 22 g carbohydrate, 2 g fiber, 11 g protein. **Diabetic Exchanges:** 1 starch, 1 very lean meat, 1 vegetable, 1 fat.

Southwestern Chicken Soup

(Pictured below)

Anne Smithson, Cary, North Carolina

The spices really liven up the flavor in this filling soup. I often double the recipe, freezing leftovers for future meals or quick lunches.

   1 can (49-1/2 ounces) chicken broth
   1 can (14-1/2 ounces) crushed tomatoes, undrained
   1 can (14-1/2 ounces) diced tomatoes, undrained
   1 pound boneless skinless chicken breasts, cut into 1/2-inch cubes
   1 large onion, chopped
1/3 cup minced fresh cilantro

   1 can (4 ounces) chopped green chilies
   1 garlic clove, minced
   1 teaspoon chili powder
   1 teaspoon ground cumin
1/2 teaspoon dried oregano
1/4 teaspoon cayenne pepper
   3 cups frozen corn, thawed
Baked tortilla chips
   1 cup (4 ounces) shredded cheddar *or* Mexican cheese blend

In a large saucepan, combine the first 12 ingredients. Bring to a boil. Reduce heat; cover and simmer for 1 hour. Add corn; cook 10 minutes longer. Top each serving with tortilla chips; sprinkle with cheese. **Yield:** 8 servings.

Mandarin Chicken Salad

(Pictured above)

Judy Sloter, Alpharetta, Georgia

I receive many compliments whenever I serve this salad. It's great to serve for brunch or at a shower.

   3 cups diced cooked chicken
   1 cup diced celery
   2 tablespoons lemon juice
   1 tablespoon finely chopped onion
3/4 cup mayonnaise
   1 can (11 ounces) mandarin oranges, drained
   1 cup seedless grapes, halved
   1 teaspoon lemon pepper
1/2 cup chopped pecans, toasted

In a medium bowl, combine first eight ingredients; mix well. Cover and chill for 1-2 hours. Fold in pecans just before serving. **Yield:** 4 servings.

equals 236 calories, 7 g fat (2 g saturated fat), 46 mg cholesterol, 184 mg sodium, 26 g carbohydrate, 2 g fiber, 18 g protein. **Diabetic Exchanges:** 2 lean meat, 1-1/2 fat, 1 fruit.

Fruity Chicken Salad

(Pictured above)

Diane Bradley, Sparta, Michigan

When served with hot rolls or muffins, this tangy salad is a terrific alternative to the usual lunchtime fare. It is also a great way to use leftover chicken or turkey.

☑ Uses less fat, sugar or salt. Includes Nutritional Analysis and Diabetic Exchanges.

- 2 cups cubed cooked chicken breast
- 2 cups cubed cantaloupe
- 2 cups cubed honeydew
- 1 can (11 ounces) mandarin oranges, drained
- 1 cup green grapes
- 1 cup halved fresh strawberries
- 1/2 cup thinly sliced celery
- 2 tablespoons finely chopped green onion
- 1/4 cup reduced-fat sour cream
- 3 tablespoons reduced-fat mayonnaise
- 1 tablespoon orange juice concentrate
- 1 tablespoon sugar
- 1/4 teaspoon celery salt
- 4 to 5 teaspoons water
Leaf lettuce
- 1/4 cup sliced almonds, toasted

In a large bowl, combine the chicken, fruit, celery and onion. In a small bowl, combine the sour cream, mayonnaise, orange juice concentrate, sugar and celery salt. Add enough water to achieve drizzling consistency.

Place lettuce on plates; top with chicken mixture. Drizzle with dressing; sprinkle with almonds. Serve immediately. **Yield:** 6 servings.

Nutritional Analysis: One serving (1-1/3 cups)

Dilled Chicken Salad

Kimberly Speta, Kennedy, New York

I usually harvest a bounty of recipe requests whenever I serve this hearty, fresh-tasting salad with its delicate dill flavor.

- 1 package (16 ounces) spiral pasta, cooked and drained
- 2 cups cubed cooked chicken
- 1 cup chopped celery
- 1/3 cup chopped onion
- 1 package (10 ounces) frozen peas, thawed
DRESSING:
- 1 envelope ranch salad dressing mix
- 2 cups (16 ounces) sour cream
- 1 cup mayonnaise
- 1 cup milk
- 3 tablespoons minced fresh dill *or* 1 tablespoon dill weed
- 1/2 teaspoon garlic salt

In a large bowl, combine the first five ingredients; mix well. Combine dressing ingredients; whisk until smooth. Pour over salad; toss to coat. Cover and refrigerate for at least 2 hours. **Yield:** 10-12 servings.

Chicken 'n' Bean Tacos

Wendy Hines, Chesnee, South Carolina

These easy-to-make tacos are great for lunch or supper any time of the year. The black beans make them filling as well as tasty!

- 1 pound boneless skinless chicken breasts, cut into bite-size pieces
- 1/2 cup chopped onion
- 2 garlic cloves, minced
- 1 can (15 ounces) black beans, undrained
- 1/4 cup minced fresh parsley
- 1 to 2 teaspoons ground cumin
- 1/4 teaspoon pepper
- 12 corn tortillas (6 inches), warmed
- 1/2 cup shredded cheddar cheese
- 1 cup chopped fresh tomatoes

In a nonstick skillet, saute the chicken, onion and garlic until chicken juices run clear. Stir in beans, parsley, cumin and pepper; heat through.

Spoon 1/3 cup down the center of each tortilla; sprinkle with cheese and tomatoes. Fold in half; serve immediately. **Yield:** 1 dozen.

Chicken Quesadillas

(Pictured below)

Linda Wetzel, Woodland Park, Colorado

These have an impressive look and taste without tricky, time-consuming preparation.

2-1/2 cups shredded cooked chicken
  2/3 cup salsa
  1/3 cup sliced green onions
  3/4 to 1 teaspoon ground cumin
  1/2 teaspoon salt
  1/2 teaspoon dried oregano
    6 flour tortillas (8 inches)
  1/4 cup butter, melted
    2 cups (8 ounces) shredded Monterey Jack cheese
Sour cream and guacamole

In a skillet, combine the first six ingredients. Cook, uncovered, over medium heat for 10 minutes or until heated through, stirring occasionally.

Brush one side of tortillas with butter. Spoon 1/3 cup chicken mixture over half of unbuttered side of each tortilla. Sprinkle with 1/3 cup cheese; fold plain side of tortilla over cheese. Place on a lightly greased baking sheet.

Bake at 475° for 10 minutes or until crisp and golden brown. Cut into wedges; serve with sour cream and guacamole. **Yield:** 6 servings.

Layered Salad

(Pictured above)

Joanne Trentadue, Racine, Wisconsin

I prepare this satisfying salad Saturday evening and serve it to my husband and sons on Sunday after a round of golf. It has a unique mix of vegetables like bean sprouts, green onions, water chestnuts and pea pods.

  4 to 5 cups shredded iceberg lettuce
    1 medium cucumber, thinly sliced
    1 cup fresh bean sprouts
    1 can (8 ounces) sliced water chestnuts, drained
  1/2 cup thinly sliced green onions
    1 pound fresh pea pods, halved
    4 cups cubed cooked chicken
    2 cups mayonnaise
    1 tablespoon sugar
    2 teaspoons curry powder
  1/2 teaspoon ground ginger
Cherry tomatoes and fresh parsley sprigs, optional

Place lettuce in the bottom of a 4-qt. glass salad bowl. Layer with cucumber, bean sprouts, water chestnuts, onions, pea pods and chicken.

In a small bowl, combine mayonnaise, sugar, curry and ginger. Spread over top of salad. Garnish with cherry tomatoes and parsley if desired. Cover and chill several hours or overnight. **Yield:** 8-10 servings.

Avocado Malibu Salad

(Pictured above)

Brenda Brinkley, Watsonville, California

One of the first things I learned when I moved here from Oregon was to make light salads like this. This one is practical, easy and delicious with a refreshing mix of fruits, chicken and seafood! Serve with crusty bread for a wonderful lunch or dinner.

        1/4 cup sour cream
        1/4 teaspoon curry powder
        1/8 teaspoon salt
          1 cup diced cooked chicken
          1 can (8 ounces) pineapple chunks, drained
        1/4 cup chopped green pepper
        1/4 cup frozen *or* canned crabmeat, drained,
             flaked and cartilage removed
          1 tablespoon diced pimientos
          2 large avocados, peeled and sliced
          2 tablespoons lemon juice
             Lettuce leaves
             Red grapes, optional

In a large bowl, combine sour cream, curry powder and salt. Add the chicken, pineapple, green pepper, crab and pimientos.

Cover and refrigerate for 1-2 hours. Just before serving, toss avocados with lemon juice. Place avocados and crab mixture on lettuce. Garnish with grapes if desired. **Yield:** 4 servings.

Peeling Avocados

Avocados are easier to peel and slice when they're ripe yet firm. To remove the peel, scoop out the flesh from each half with a large metal spoon, staying close to the flesh. Slice and dip in lemon or lime juice to prevent browning.

Southwestern Salad

(Pictured below)

Margaret Yost, Casstown, Ohio

We have five children who love Mexican food, salads and chicken. So I combined all three to make this crunchy main dish. There's no groaning from anyone when I set it on the table.

- 1/3 cup Thousand Island salad dressing
- 1/3 cup salsa
- 1/4 cup sour cream
- 1 teaspoon seasoned salt
- 1 teaspoon garlic powder
- 1/2 teaspoon lemon-pepper seasoning
- 1/4 teaspoon cayenne pepper
- 1 pound boneless skinless chicken breasts, cut into 1/4-inch strips
- 1 tablespoon canola oil
- 1 *each* medium sweet red and green pepper, cut into 1/4-inch strips
- 2 teaspoons lime juice
- 12 cups torn romaine
- 1-1/2 cups (6 ounces) shredded cheddar cheese
- 1 cup shredded red cabbage
- 1 medium tomato, chopped
- 1 medium carrot, grated
- Baked tortilla chips

In a small bowl, combine the salad dressing, salsa and sour cream. Cover and refrigerate until serving.

Combine the seasonings; sprinkle over chicken. In a nonstick skillet, saute chicken in oil for 6 minutes. Add peppers; saute 2-3 minutes longer or until chicken juices run clear. Drizzle with lime juice; keep warm.

In a large bowl, toss the romaine, cheese, cabbage, tomato and carrot. Add chicken mixture. Serve over chips; drizzle with dressing. **Yield:** 8 servings.

Broccoli Chicken Braid

(Pictured above)

Diane Wampler, Morristown, Tennessee

I work outside the home, so I appreciate recipes like this that are fast and delicious. My family gobbles up this tasty braid, and I'm happy to sneak in some vegetables that my children will eat.

- 2 cups chopped cooked chicken
- 1 cup chopped fresh broccoli florets
- 1 cup (4 ounces) shredded cheddar cheese
- 1/4 cup chopped green pepper
- 1/4 cup chopped sweet red pepper
- 1 garlic clove, minced
- 1 teaspoon dill weed
- 1/4 teaspoon salt
- 1/2 cup mayonnaise
- 2 tubes (8 ounces *each*) refrigerated crescent rolls
- 1 egg white, lightly beaten
- 2 tablespoons slivered almonds

In a bowl, combine the first eight ingredients. Stir in mayonnaise. Unroll both tubes of crescent roll dough into one long rectangle on an ungreased baking sheet. Roll into a 15-in. x 12-in. rectangle, sealing seams and perforations.

Spoon chicken mixture down center third of dough. On each long side, cut eight strips about 3-1/2 in. into the center. Bring one strip from each side over filling and pinch ends to seal; repeat. Brush with egg white. Sprinkle with almonds.

Bake at 375° for 15-20 minutes or until the filling is heated through and the top is golden brown. **Yield:** 8 servings.

Fruit 'n' Tortellini Salad

(Pictured below)

Vicky McClain, St. Albans, Vermont

Being from Vermont, the nation's leading maple syrup-producing state, I use pure maple syrup for a special sweet taste. By adding chicken, the salad makes a light main course.

- 1 package (9 ounces) refrigerated cheese tortellini
- 1 can (11 ounces) mandarin oranges, drained
- 1 medium grapefruit, peeled and sectioned
- 1 medium lemon, peeled and sectioned
- 2 kiwifruit, peeled and sliced
- 1 cup halved seedless red grapes
- 2 cups cubed cooked chicken
- 1/2 cup maple syrup
- 1/2 cup orange juice
- 1/2 cup cashews

Cook tortellini according to package directions. Drain and rinse with cold water. In a large bowl, combine the tortellini, fruit and chicken.

In a small bowl, whisk the syrup and orange juice; pour over salad and toss to coat. Cover and refrigerate for at least 1 hour. Sprinkle with cashews just before serving. **Yield:** 6-8 servings.

Mexican Chicken Corn Chowder

(Pictured above)

Susan Garoutte, Georgetown, Texas

I like to make this creamy soup when company comes to visit. Its zippy flavor is full of Southwestern flair. My family enjoys dipping slices of homemade bread in this chowder to soak up every bite!

- 1-1/2 pounds boneless skinless chicken breasts
- 1/2 cup chopped onion
- 1 to 2 garlic cloves, minced
- 3 tablespoons butter
- 2 chicken bouillon cubes
- 1 cup hot water
- 1/2 to 1 teaspoon ground cumin
- 2 cups half-and-half cream
- 2 cups (8 ounces) shredded Monterey Jack cheese
- 1 can (16 ounces) cream-style corn
- 1 can (4 ounces) chopped green chilies, undrained
- 1/4 to 1 teaspoon hot pepper sauce
- 1 medium tomato, chopped

Fresh cilantro, optional

Cut chicken into bite-size pieces. In a Dutch oven, cook chicken, onion and garlic in butter until chicken juices run clear. Dissolve the bouillon in hot water. Add to pan along with cumin; bring to a boil. Reduce heat; cover and simmer for 5 minutes.

Add cream, cheese, corn, chilies and hot pepper sauce. Cook and stir over low heat until the cheese is melted. Stir in tomato. Serve immediately; garnish with cilantro if desired. **Yield:** 6-8 servings (2 quarts).

Nutty Chicken Pita Sandwiches

(Pictured at right)

Glenda Schwarz, Morden, Manitoba

When company is coming for lunch, this is my favorite sandwich to make, since it looks and tastes a bit fancy. Even kids like it because of the crunchy nuts and creamy filling.

- 1 package (8 ounces) cream cheese, softened
- 3 tablespoons milk
- 1 tablespoon lemon juice
- 2 cups cubed cooked chicken
- 1/2 cup chopped green pepper
- 2 tablespoons chopped green onions
- 1 teaspoon ground mustard
- 1/2 teaspoon dried thyme
- 1/2 teaspoon salt
- 1/8 teaspoon pepper
- 1/4 cup chopped walnuts
- 3 large pita breads, halved

Alfalfa sprouts, optional

In a mixing bowl, beat cream cheese, milk and lemon juice until smooth. Stir in the chicken, green pepper, onions, mustard, thyme, salt and pepper; refrigerate. Just before serving, stir in walnuts. Spoon about 1/2 cup filling into each pita half. Top with alfalfa sprouts if desired. **Yield:** 3-6 servings.

Mandarin Pasta Salad

Kathleen Dougherty, Williamsville, Illinois

I developed this recipe when I was asked to bring a salad to a birthday party for my husband's grandfather.

- 1 package (1 pound) angel hair pasta *or* thin spaghetti, broken into thirds
- 1 pound boneless skinless chicken breasts, cut into 1-inch cubes
- 2 garlic cloves, minced
- 2 tablespoons butter
- 1-1/2 teaspoons seasoned salt
- 1 can (8 ounces) sliced water chestnuts, drained
- 2 cans (11 ounces *each*) mandarin oranges
- 1 package (6 ounces) frozen snow peas, thawed and drained
- 2 cups sliced fresh mushrooms
- 2 cups shredded carrots
- 2 bunches green onions, sliced

DRESSING:
- 2/3 cup vegetable oil
- 1/2 cup white wine vinegar
- 3 tablespoons soy sauce
- 1 garlic clove, minced
- 1 tablespoon sugar
- 1 tablespoon honey
- 1/2 teaspoon ground ginger
- 3 tablespoons sesame seeds, toasted

Cook pasta according to package directions. Drain and rinse with cold water; set aside. In a large skillet, saute chicken and garlic in butter until chicken juices run clear; sprinkle with seasoned salt. Remove with a slotted spoon; set aside.

In the same skillet, saute water chestnuts for 2-3 minutes. Drain oranges, reserving 1/2 cup juice. In a large serving bowl, combine oranges, pasta, chicken, water chestnuts, peas, mushrooms, carrots and onions.

In a jar with a tight-fitting lid, combine the oil, vinegar, soy sauce, garlic, sugar, honey, ginger and reserved mandarin orange juice; shake well. Pour over pasta mixture and toss. Sprinkle with sesame seeds. Refrigerate until serving. **Yield:** 20-25 servings.

Open Sesame

Sesame seed is versatile and can be used in many of the same ways as nuts. The seed has a nutty, sweet aroma with a milk-like, buttery taste. Toasting sesame seeds will intensify their flavor.

Dijon Chicken Salad

Raymond Sienko, Hawleyville, Connecticut

This salad is my most-requested recipe because it has a perfect combination of flavors.

     4 cups cubed cooked chicken
     1 cup sliced celery
     1 cup seedless green grapes, halved
     1 cup seedless red grapes, halved
   1/4 cup chopped dried apricots
   1/4 cup sliced green onions
   3/4 cup mayonnaise
     2 tablespoons honey
     1 tablespoon Dijon mustard
   1/2 teaspoon salt
   1/8 teaspoon pepper
Lettuce leaves
   1/2 cup sliced almonds

In a bowl, combine the first six ingredients. In a small bowl, combine mayonnaise, honey, mustard, salt and pepper; mix well. Stir into chicken mixture. Cover and refrigerate until serving. Serve on a lettuce-lined plate. Sprinkle with almonds. **Yield:** 6 servings.

Almond Chicken Salad

(Pictured above)

Kathy Kittell, Lenexa, Kansas

My mother used to prepare this salad for an evening meal during the hot summer months. It also serves well as a delicious but quick luncheon or potluck dish.

       4 cups cubed cooked chicken
   1-1/2 cups seedless green grapes, halved
       1 cup chopped celery
     3/4 cup sliced green onions
       3 hard-cooked eggs, chopped
     1/2 cup mayonnaise
     1/4 cup sour cream
       1 tablespoon prepared mustard
       1 teaspoon salt
     1/2 teaspoon pepper
     1/4 teaspoon onion powder
     1/4 teaspoon celery salt
     1/8 teaspoon ground mustard
     1/8 teaspoon paprika
     1/2 cup slivered almonds, toasted
       1 kiwifruit, peeled and sliced, optional

In a large bowl, combine the chicken, grapes, celery, onions and hard-cooked eggs. In another bowl, combine the mayonnaise, sour cream, mustard, salt, pepper, onion powder, celery salt, ground mustard and paprika; stir until smooth. Pour over the chicken mixture and toss gently.

Stir in almonds and serve immediately, or refrigerate and add the almonds just before serving. Garnish with kiwi if desired. **Yield:** 6-8 servings.

White Chili

Kevin Gardiner, Eutaw, Alabama

This recipe was given to me by a friend who got it from another friend. The day after I served it, someone called me for the recipe, too.

✓ Uses less fat, sugar or salt. Includes Nutritional Analysis and Diabetic Exchanges.

       2 pounds dried great northern beans
   1-1/2 cups diced onion
       1 tablespoon vegetable oil
       1 tablespoon ground oregano
       2 teaspoons ground cumin
   1-1/2 teaspoons seasoned salt
     1/2 teaspoon cayenne pepper
   4-1/2 quarts fat-free reduced-sodium chicken broth
       2 garlic cloves, minced
       8 boneless skinless chicken breast halves, cubed
       2 cans (4 ounces *each*) chopped green chilies

Place beans in a saucepan; cover with water and bring to a boil. Boil 2 minutes. Remove from heat. Soak 1 hour; drain and rinse.

In an 8-qt. Dutch oven, saute onion in oil until tender. Combine seasonings; add half to Dutch oven. Saute 1 minute. Add beans, broth and garlic; bring to a boil. Reduce heat; simmer 2 hours.

Coat chicken with remaining seasoning mixture; place in a 15-in. x 10-in. x 1-in. baking pan. Bake at

350° for 15 minutes or until juices run clear; add to beans. Stir in chilies. Simmer 1-1/2 to 2 hours. **Yield:** 20 servings.

Nutritional Analysis: One 1-cup serving equals 169 calories, 365 mg sodium, 29 mg cholesterol, 17 g carbohydrate, 18 g protein, 3 g fat. **Diabetic Exchanges:** 2 lean meat, 1 starch.

Picnic Chicken Pitas

(Pictured below)

Marla Brenneman, Goshen, Indiana

A mustard-flavored dressing coats the colorful combination of chicken, broccoli, tomatoes and bacon. It's great for a picnic because you can assemble the sandwiches right at the picnic site.

✓ Uses less fat, sugar or salt. Includes Nutritional Analysis and Diabetic Exchanges.

1 package (10 ounces) frozen broccoli florets, cooked and drained
2 cups shredded cooked chicken
1 cup (4 ounces) shredded reduced-fat cheddar cheese
1 medium tomato, chopped
1/4 cup fat-free mayonnaise
2 tablespoons prepared mustard
1/2 teaspoon salt, optional
1/8 teaspoon pepper
4 pita breads (6 inches), halved
4 bacon strips, cooked and crumbled, optional

In a large bowl, combine the broccoli, chicken, cheese and tomato. In a small bowl, combine the mayonnaise, mustard, salt if desired and pepper; pour over the broccoli mixture and toss to coat. Spoon about 3/4 cup into each pita half; top with bacon if desired. **Yield:** 4 servings.

Nutritional Analysis: One serving (prepared without salt and bacon) equals 320 calories, 725 mg sodium, 48 mg cholesterol, 41 g carbohydrate, 26 g protein, 5 g fat. **Diabetic Exchanges:** 3 lean meat, 2-1/2 starch.

2 Skillet & Stovetop Suppers

Lime Ginger Chicken

(Pictured at left)

Patti Billet, Missoula, Montana

I find it very relaxing to spend time in my kitchen trying out new recipes. This particular recipe is one of my favorites—it won first prize in a statewide contest! The salsa is a zippy addition and has tons of fresh ingredients like plum tomatoes, green pepper and cilantro.

✓ Uses less fat, sugar or salt. Includes Nutritional Analysis and Diabetic Exchanges.

- 1/3 cup fresh lime juice
- 3 garlic cloves, minced
- 1/2 teaspoon ground ginger
- 1/2 teaspoon dried red pepper flakes
- 1/4 teaspoon salt, optional
- 4 boneless skinless chicken breast halves, cut into 1-inch strips

SALSA:
- 2 cups diced fresh plum tomatoes
- 1 cup diced green pepper
- 1/2 cup diced red onion
- 1 tablespoon chopped fresh cilantro
- 1 tablespoon olive oil
- 1 tablespoon fresh lime juice
- 2 garlic cloves, minced
- 1/4 teaspoon salt, optional

In a glass bowl, combine lime juice, minced garlic, ginger, red pepper and salt if desired. Add the chicken and toss lightly. Cover and refrigerate for 2-4 hours.

Meanwhile, combine all of the salsa ingredients; cover and refrigerate until serving. Drain chicken and discard the marinade. Cook in a large nonstick skillet until no longer pink, about 10 minutes. Serve with salsa. **Yield:** 4 servings.

The Skinny on Chicken

Chicken can be a healthy choice for your weekday menus. But you can make it even healthier.

Try preparing the boneless skinless chicken breasts or thighs using reduced-fat cooking methods like stir-frying and grilling.

Nutritional Analysis: One serving (prepared without salt) equals 250 calories, 80 mg sodium, 73 mg cholesterol, 20 g carbohydrate, 31 g protein, 7 g fat. **Diabetic Exchanges:** 3 lean meat, 3 vegetable.

Sunflower Chicken

Lori Daniels, Beverly, West Virginia

This chicken stir-fry gets a nice crunch from sunflower kernels, carrots, celery and broccoli. It's full of color and flavor, making it one of my family's all-time favorites!

✓ Uses less fat, sugar or salt. Includes Nutritional Analysis and Diabetic Exchanges.

- 1 pound boneless skinless chicken breasts, cut into strips
- 3 medium carrots, sliced
- 2 celery ribs, sliced
- 1 medium onion, chopped
- 1 can (4 ounces) mushroom stems and pieces, drained
- 1 medium sweet red pepper, julienned
- 4 cups broccoli florets
- 1/4 cup sunflower kernels, toasted
- 1/4 teaspoon salt-free seasoning blend
- 1/4 teaspoon garlic powder
- 3 tablespoons cornstarch
- 1 can (14-1/2 ounces) reduced-sodium chicken broth

Hot cooked rice, optional

In a skillet coated with nonstick cooking spray, stir-fry the chicken until no longer pink. Add the carrots, celery, onion, mushrooms, red pepper, broccoli, sunflower kernels, salt-free seasoning blend and garlic powder; stir-fry for 5-6 minutes or until the vegetables are tender.

Combine cornstarch and broth until smooth; add to skillet. bring to a boil; cook and stir for 2 minutes or until thickened. Serve over rice if desired. **Yield:** 6 servings.

Nutritional Analysis: One serving (calculated without rice) equals 190 calories, 183 mg sodium, 43 mg cholesterol, 16 g carbohydrate, 20 g protein, 5 g fat. **Diabetic Exchanges:** 3 very lean meat, 1 starch, 1/2 fat.

Creamy Braised Chicken

(Pictured below)

Pat Patty, Spring, Texas

A smooth and delicate cream sauce gives a special taste to these tender chicken breasts accompanied by sweet pearl onions and sauteed mushrooms.

✓ Uses less fat, sugar or salt. Includes Nutritional Analysis and Diabetic Exchanges.

- 1/2 **pound pearl onions**
- 1 **cup thinly sliced onion**
- 1/2 **cup thinly sliced carrot**
- 1/2 **cup thinly sliced celery**
- 1 **tablespoon plus 2 teaspoons butter,** *divided*
- 6 **boneless skinless chicken breast halves (1-1/2 pounds)**
- 1 **cup chardonnay** *or* **other dry white wine** *or* **reduced-sodium chicken broth**
- 1-1/3 **cups reduced-sodium chicken broth**
- 1 **tablespoon minced fresh parsley**
- 1 **teaspoon salt**
- 1 **teaspoon dried thyme**
- 1/8 **teaspoon white pepper**
- 1 **bay leaf**
- 3 **tablespoons all-purpose flour**
- 1/2 **cup fat-free evaporated milk**
- 1/2 **pound fresh mushrooms, quartered**

In a Dutch oven or large kettle, bring 6 cups water to a boil. Add pearl onions; boil for 3 minutes. Drain and rinse in cold water; peel and set aside. In the same pan, saute sliced onion, carrot and celery in 1 tablespoon butter until tender. Remove the vegetables and set aside.

Add chicken to the pan; brown on both sides. Remove and keep warm. Add wine or broth; simmer until reduced to 1/2 cup. Stir in broth and seasonings. Return chicken to pan; cover and simmer for 5 minutes or until juices run clear. Remove chicken to a serving platter; keep warm.

Combine flour and milk until smooth; gradually stir into pan. Bring to a boil; cook and stir for 2 minutes or until thickened. Return vegetables to pan. Remove from the heat; cover and set aside.

In a nonstick skillet, saute reserved pearl onions in remaining butter until tender. Remove and set aside. In the same pan, saute mushrooms until tender. Add the onions and mushrooms to serving platter. Discard bay leaf from sauce; spoon over chicken and vegetables. **Yield:** 6 servings.

Nutritional Analysis: One serving (1 chicken breast half with 2/3 cup sauce) equals 273 calories, 5 g fat (3 g saturated fat), 75 mg cholesterol, 748 mg sodium, 18 g carbohydrate, 2 g fiber, 31 g protein. **Diabetic Exchanges:** 3 lean meat, 3 vegetable, 1/2 fat.

Pine Nut Chicken

Wanda Holoubek, Omaha, Nebraska

The crunch of pine nuts add great flavor and texture to this light dish. My family loves it! You can also use almonds to give this dish the same great taste.

- 3/4 **cup all-purpose flour**
- 1/4 **teaspoon salt**
- 1/8 **teaspoon pepper**
- 2 **eggs**
- 6 **boneless skinless chicken breast halves (1-1/2 pounds)**
- 2 **cups chopped pine nuts** *or* **almonds**
- 1/3 **cup butter**

Place flour, salt and pepper in a shallow bowl. Beat eggs in another shallow bowl. Flatten chicken to 1/2-in. thickness. Coat with flour mixture; dip into eggs. Pat the nuts firmly onto both sides of the chicken.

In a large skillet over medium heat, cook the chicken in butter for 4-5 minutes on each side or until browned and juices run clear. **Yield:** 4-6 servings.

Moist Chicken

If using skin-on chicken, remove the skin after cooking instead of before. This will help allow the chicken to stay moist while it cooks.

Chicken and Dumplings

(Pictured above)

Willa Govoro, St. Clair, Missouri

On Sundays, Mom set our big round oak table with a snowy white cloth and her fine dishes and tableware. On the old wood stove, pushed way back to simmer slowly, was a big pot of chicken and dumplings in a thick gravy.

   1 **cup all-purpose flour**
   2 **broiler/fryer chickens (2-1/2 to 3 pounds *each*), cut up**
   2 **tablespoons vegetable oil**
   3 **celery ribs, cut into 1-inch pieces**
   3 **medium carrots, cut into 1-inch pieces**
1/4 **cup chopped fresh parsley**
   2 **teaspoons salt**
   1 **teaspoon garlic powder**
   1 **teaspoon dried thyme**
1/2 **teaspoon pepper**
   8 **to 12 cups water**
DUMPLINGS:
   2 **cups all-purpose flour**
   2 **teaspoons baking powder**
   2 **eggs, beaten**

GRAVY:
1/4 **cup all-purpose flour**
1/2 **cup water**

Place flour in a bowl or bag; add the chicken pieces and dredge or shake to coat. In a large skillet, brown chicken in oil; drain. Place in an 8-qt. Dutch oven.

Add the celery, carrots, parsley, salt, garlic powder, thyme and pepper. Add enough water to cover chicken; bring to a boil. Reduce the heat; cover and simmer until the chicken is almost tender, about 45-50 minutes.

Remove 1 cup of broth to use for dumplings; cool, then add flour, baking powder and eggs. Mix well to form a stiff batter; drop by tablespoonfuls into simmering broth. Cover and simmer for 15-20 minutes. Remove chicken and dumplings to a serving dish and keep warm.

For gravy, remove 4 cups broth and vegetables to a large saucepan; bring to a boil. Combine flour and water; mix well. Stir into vegetable mixture. Cook over medium heat, stirring constantly, until thickened and bubbly. Pour over chicken and dumplings. Serve immediately. **Yield:** 6-8 servings.

Editor's Note: Any remaining chicken broth can be frozen for future use.

Chicken Fried Rice

Kathy Hoyt, Maplecrest, New York

I rely on a fried rice mix to start this speedy skillet supper. It makes the most of leftover cooked chicken and a can of crunchy water chestnuts.

- 1 package (6.2 ounces) fried rice mix
- 2 cups cubed cooked chicken
- 1-1/2 cups cooked broccoli florets
- 1 can (8 ounces) sliced water chestnuts, drained
- 1 cup (4 ounces) shredded mozzarella cheese

Cook rice according to the package directions. Stir in the cooked chicken, broccoli and water chestnuts; heat through. Sprinkle with mozzarella cheese. **Yield:** 4 servings.

Southern Chicken Roll-Ups

(Pictured above)

Catherine Darr, Charlotte, Arkansas

This is one of my favorite ways to cook chicken because it tastes so good and doesn't take long to prepare. I like to serve these roll-ups over rice.

✓ Uses less fat, sugar or salt. Includes Nutritional Analysis and Diabetic Exchanges.

- 6 boneless skinless chicken breast halves (1-1/2 pounds)
- 6 slices reduced-fat Swiss cheese
- 3 tablespoons all-purpose flour
- 1/2 teaspoon pepper
- 2 tablespoons margarine
- 3/4 cup chicken reduced-sodium broth
- 1/2 teaspoon dried oregano

Flatten chicken to 1/4-in. thickness. Place a cheese slice on each; roll up jelly-roll style. In a shallow bowl, combine the flour and pepper; add the chicken and roll to coat.

In a skillet over medium heat, cook chicken in butter until browned, about 10 minutes, turning frequently. Add broth and oregano; bring to a boil. Reduce heat; simmer for 12-14 minutes or until chicken juices run clear. **Yield:** 6 servings.

Nutritional Analysis: One serving equals 284 calories, 157 mg sodium, 94 mg cholesterol, 4 g carbohydrate, 36 g protein, 13 g fat. **Diabetic Exchanges:** 4 lean meat, 1/2 starch, 1/2 fat.

Cashew Chicken Stir-Fry

(Pictured below)

Vicki Hirschfeld, Hartland, Wisconsin

For me, the hardest part of making this quick dish is keeping the cashews in the cupboard! My family loves those crunchy nuts, and this dish!

- 2 cups chicken broth, *divided*
- 1/4 cup cornstarch
- 3 tablespoons soy sauce
- 1/2 teaspoon ground ginger

1 pound boneless skinless chicken breasts,
   cut into 1/2-inch strips
2 garlic cloves, minced
1/2 cup thinly sliced carrots
1/2 cup sliced celery (1/2-inch pieces)
3 cups broccoli florets
1 cup fresh *or* frozen snow peas
1-1/2 cups cashews
Hot cooked rice, optional

In a skillet, heat 3 tablespoons of broth. Meanwhile, in a bowl, combine the cornstarch, soy sauce, ginger and remaining broth until smooth; set aside.

Add chicken to the skillet; stir-fry over medium heat until no longer pink, about 3-5 minutes. Remove with a slotted spoon and keep warm. Add garlic, carrots and celery to skillet; stir-fry for 3 minutes. Add broccoli and peas; stir-fry for 4-5 minutes or until crisp-tender.

Stir broth mixture; add to the skillet with the chicken. Cook and stir for 2 minutes. Stir in cashews. Serve over rice if desired. **Yield:** 4 servings.

Chili-Spiced Chicken Breasts

Stacey Nutt, Lockney, Texas

Spicing up dinnertime at my house is a snap when I make this zippy chicken dish. The mix of chili powder, jalapeno and cayenne pepper perks up the poultry perfectly.

3/4 teaspoon chili powder
1/2 teaspoon salt
1/2 teaspoon ground cumin
1/4 teaspoon garlic powder
1/8 to 1/4 teaspoon cayenne pepper
4 boneless skinless chicken breast halves
   (4 ounces *each*)
1 teaspoon canola oil
1/4 cup chopped green onions
1 jalapeno pepper, seeded and finely chopped
1 garlic clove, minced
1 can (14-1/2 ounces) diced tomatoes,
   undrained
1 teaspoon cornstarch
2 teaspoons water

Combine the first five ingredients; rub over chicken. In a nonstick skillet, brown chicken in oil on both sides. Add onions, jalapeno and garlic; saute for 1 minute. Add tomatoes; bring to a boil.

Reduce heat; cover and simmer for 15-20 minutes or until chicken juices run clear. Remove chicken and keep warm. In a small bowl, combine cornstarch and water until smooth; stir into tomato mixture. Bring to a boil; cook and stir for 1 minute or until slightly thickened. Serve over chicken. **Yield:** 4 servings.

Editor's Note: When cutting or seeding hot peppers, use rubber or plastic gloves to protect your hands. Avoid touching your face.

Bow Tie Lemon Chicken

(Pictured above)

Rebecca Snapp, Cynthiana, Kentucky

The zesty flavor of lemon brightens every bite of this creamy chicken and pasta dish. With two sons and a farmer husband who has a second full-time job, it's a good thing I have a collection of speedy recipes.

4-2/3 cups uncooked bow tie pasta
12 ounces boneless skinless chicken breasts,
   cut into 1-inch strips
1/2 teaspoon lemon-pepper seasoning
2 garlic cloves, minced
1 tablespoon canola oil
1 cup chicken broth
1 cup frozen peas, thawed
2/3 cup shredded carrots
1/4 cup cubed cream cheese
2 teaspoons lemon juice
1/2 teaspoon salt
1/3 cup shredded Parmesan cheese

Cook pasta according to package directions. Meanwhile, sprinkle chicken with lemon-pepper. In a large nonstick skillet, stir-fry chicken and garlic in oil until chicken juices run clear. Remove and keep warm.

Add broth, peas, carrots, cream cheese and lemon juice to the skillet; cook and stir until cheese is melted. Drain pasta. Add pasta, chicken and salt to vegetable mixture; heat through. Sprinkle with Parmesan cheese. **Yield:** 4 servings.

Chicken Rice Skillet

(Pictured above)

Jan Balata, Kilkenny, Minnesota

Pleasant seasonings and plenty of vegetables highlight this traditional chicken and rice pairing. Leftovers are great reheated in the microwave.

      4 **boneless skinless chicken breast halves (1 pound)**
      2 **tablespoons olive oil**
      2 **celery ribs, chopped**
      4 **green onions, thinly sliced**
  1/2 **cup chopped sweet red pepper**
  1/2 **cup chopped sweet yellow pepper**
      2 **cups frozen green beans, thawed**
      1 **jar (4-1/2 ounces) sliced mushrooms, drained**
      1 **can (14-1/2 ounces) chicken broth**
  1/4 **cup water**
      3 **garlic cloves, minced**
  1/2 **teaspoon salt**
  1/4 **teaspoon lemon-pepper seasoning**
  1/8 **teaspoon garlic powder**
  1/8 **teaspoon pepper**
      2 **cups uncooked instant rice**

In a large skillet over medium heat, brown chicken in oil for about 4 minutes on each side or until almost tender. Add celery, onions and peppers; cook until vegetables are crisp-tender. Stir in beans and mushrooms; cook until chicken juices run clear.

Stir in the broth, water and seasonings. Bring to a boil. Stir in rice; cover and remove from the heat. Let stand for 5 minutes or until rice is tender; fluff rice with a fork. **Yield:** 4 servings.

Making Lighter Chicken

To cut down on fat and calories, use nonstick cooking spray rather than vegetable oil in recipes like Parmesan Chicken on page 31. Using nonstick cooking spray also works great to prevent sticking.

Jambalaya Pasta

Christy Leonhard, Durham, North Carolina

I use bay leaves often in my cooking. They add wonderful flavor, but remember to remove them before serving!

✓ Uses less fat, sugar or salt. Includes Nutritional Analysis and Diabetic Exchanges.

- 1/2 cup *each* chopped onion, green pepper and sweet red pepper
- 1/3 cup chopped celery
- 1 tablespoon reduced-fat margarine
- 1 can (14-1/2 ounces) no-salt-added Italian diced *or* stewed tomatoes, undrained
- 1 can (14-1/2 ounces) reduced-sodium chicken broth
- 2/3 cup sliced fresh mushrooms
- 1 teaspoon dried basil *or* thyme
- 3 to 4 bay leaves
- 1/4 teaspoon garlic powder
- 1/4 teaspoon pepper
- 1/8 teaspoon cayenne pepper
- 8 ounces spiral pasta
- 2 cups cubed cooked chicken

In a skillet, saute onion, peppers and celery in butter until tender. Stir in tomatoes, broth, mushrooms and seasonings. Bring to a boil; reduce heat. Cover and simmer for 15-20 minutes.

Meanwhile, cook the pasta according to package directions. Add chicken to the tomato mixture and heat through. Drain pasta; add to chicken mixture. Discard bay leaves. **Yield:** 8 servings (2 quarts).

Nutritional Analysis: One serving equals 167 calories, 62 mg sodium, 22 mg cholesterol, 25 g carbohydrate, 10 g protein, 3 g fat. **Diabetic Exchanges:** 1-1/2 vegetable, 1 starch, 1 lean meat.

Parmesan Chicken

Molly Hall, San Ramon, California

This dish is moist and pretty to serve. My kids love the crispy coating and are happy when this is on our table.

- 4 boneless skinless chicken breast halves (1 pound)
- 1/2 cup seasoned bread crumbs
- 1/4 cup grated Parmesan cheese
- 1/2 teaspoon dried basil
- 1 egg
- 1 tablespoon butter
- 1 tablespoon vegetable oil

Flatten chicken to 1/4-in. thickness. In a shallow bowl, combine bread crumbs, Parmesan cheese and basil. In another bowl, beat the egg. Dip chicken into egg, then coat with crumb mixture. In a large skillet, cook the chicken in butter and oil over medium heat for 3-5 minutes on each side or until the juices run clear. **Yield:** 4 servings.

Tarragon Skillet Chicken

(Pictured below)

Sarah Patterson, Little Rock, Arkansas

Broilers are the leading farm product in our state, so chicken is a staple on many dinner tables here. I've prepared this recipe several times, and it always gets rave reviews.

- 1-1/2 pounds boneless skinless chicken breast halves
- Salt and pepper to taste
- 1 teaspoon lemon-pepper seasoning
- 1/4 cup butter
- 2 tablespoons minced green onions
- 1 cup heavy whipping cream
- 2 tablespoons lemon juice
- 1 teaspoon dried tarragon
- Hot cooked rice

Pound chicken to 1/4-in. thickness; cut each half into three pieces. Season with salt, pepper and lemon-pepper. In a large skillet, saute a third of the chicken at a time in butter until browned and no longer pink. Remove and keep warm.

In the same skillet, saute onions until tender. Add cream, lemon juice and tarragon; bring to a boil. Cook and stir until thickened, about 5-6 minutes. Serve over chicken with rice. **Yield:** 4 servings.

Southern Sunday Chicken

(Pictured below)

Maurine Seavers, Oliver Springs, Tennessee

Southern fried chicken is a tradition here, but I created this recipe as a substitute. My husband thinks it's wonderful.

✓ Uses less fat, sugar or salt. Includes Nutritional Analysis and Diabetic Exchanges.

```
1/2  cup all-purpose flour
  1  teaspoon salt, optional
  1  teaspoon paprika
1/4 to 1/2 teaspoon dried thyme
1/4  teaspoon celery seed
1/4  teaspoon pepper
1/8  teaspoon garlic powder
  4  boneless skinless chicken breast halves
       (1 pound)
  2  teaspoons margarine
1/4  cup chopped onion
1/4  cup chopped celery
  3  fresh mushrooms, sliced
  1  can (14-1/2 ounces) reduced-sodium chicken
       broth
  3  tablespoons all-purpose flour
  1  cup evaporated fat-free milk
Hot cooked noodles
```

In a large resealable bag, combine the first seven ingredients. Cut chicken pieces into thirds; place in the bag and shake to coat. In a large nonstick skillet, melt butter. Brown chicken on all sides; remove and keep warm. Add onion, celery and mushrooms; cook until tender. Return chicken to the pan; add broth. Cover and simmer for 15 minutes.

In a small bowl, whisk flour and milk until smooth. Add to pan; cook and stir for 2 minutes or until thickened and bubbly. Serve over noodles. **Yield:** 4 servings.

Nutritional Analysis: One serving (prepared without salt and calculated without noodles) equals 273 calories, 183 mg sodium, 67 mg cholesterol, 27 g carbohydrate, 32 g protein, 4 g fat. **Diabetic Exchanges:** 3 very lean meat, 1-1/2 vegetable, 1 starch.

Mexican Chicken and Rice

(Pictured above)

Cindy Gage, Blair, Nebraska

On days I get home late from the hospital, I'm glad this main dish comes together easily in one skillet. Sometimes, I make it ahead in the morning and refrigerate. It's so quick to just sprinkle on the cheese and reheat it for dinner.

```
  2  pounds boneless skinless chicken breasts,
       cut into 1-inch pieces
  1  medium green pepper, chopped
  1  small onion, chopped
  2  tablespoons vegetable oil
  1  can (8-3/4 ounces) whole kernel corn,
       drained
  1  cup chicken broth
  1  cup salsa
1/2 to 1 teaspoon salt
1/2 to 1 teaspoon chili powder, optional
```

1/4 teaspoon pepper
1-1/2 cups uncooked instant rice
1/2 to 1 cup shredded cheddar cheese

In a large skillet, saute the chicken, green pepper and onion in oil until chicken juices run clear and vegetables are crisp-tender. Add the corn, broth, salsa, salt, chili powder if desired and pepper; bring to a boil.

Stir in the rice; cover and remove from the heat. Let stand for 5 minutes. Fluff with a fork. Sprinkle with cheese. Cover and let stand for 2 minutes or until cheese is melted. **Yield:** 6 servings.

Chicken with Herb Sauce

Irene Cooney, Manheim, Pennsylvania

My grandmother gave me the recipe for these moist golden chicken breasts topped with a tangy butter sauce made with chives, parsley and basil. It's simple but very good.

    4 boneless skinless chicken breast halves
1/2 teaspoon salt
1/4 teaspoon pepper
    2 tablespoons butter, *divided*
    2 tablespoons olive oil, *divided*
1/2 cup chicken broth
    2 tablespoons minced chives
    2 tablespoons minced fresh parsley
    2 teaspoons lime juice
    1 teaspoon minced fresh basil
    1 teaspoon Dijon mustard

Place the chicken breasts between two sheets of waxed paper; flatten evenly with a mallet. Sprinkle both sides with salt and pepper. In a large skillet, heat 1 tablespoon each of butter and oil; cook chicken over medium-high heat for about 6 minutes on each side or until juices run clear. Remove and keep warm.

Stir broth, chives, parsley, lime juice, basil, mustard and remaining butter and oil into drippings; cook and stir until butter is melted. Serve over chicken. **Yield:** 4 servings.

Orange Walnut Chicken

(*Pictured at right*)

TerryAnn Moore, Haddon Township, New Jersey

For an impressive main dish that's not tricky to prepare, try this mouth-watering chicken. With orange juice concentrate, orange juice, lemon juice and marmalade, the pretty sauce has a zesty taste.

    3 tablespoons orange juice concentrate
    3 tablespoons vegetable oil, *divided*

    1 tablespoon soy sauce
    1 garlic clove, minced
    4 boneless skinless chicken breast halves
1/2 cup coarsely chopped walnuts
    1 tablespoon butter
    4 green onions, thinly sliced, *divided*
1/2 cup orange marmalade
1/2 cup orange juice
1/4 cup lemon juice
    2 tablespoons honey
    1 to 2 tablespoons grated orange peel
    2 to 3 teaspoons grated lemon peel
1/2 teaspoon salt
1/8 teaspoon pepper
Hot cooked rice

In a large resealable plastic bag, combine orange juice concentrate, 2 tablespoons oil, soy sauce and garlic. Add chicken; seal bag and turn to coat. Refrigerate for 2-3 hours. Remove chicken; reserve marinade. In a skillet, cook chicken in remaining oil until the chicken juices run clear.

Meanwhile, in a saucepan, saute the walnuts in butter until lightly browned; remove and set aside. Set aside 1/4 cup green onions for garnish. Add remaining onions to saucepan; saute until tender. Add reserved marinade and the next eight ingredients. Bring to a rolling boil; boil for 2 minutes.

Reduce heat; simmer, uncovered, for 5-10 minutes or until sauce reaches desired consistency. Serve chicken over rice; top with sauce and reserved walnuts and onions. **Yield:** 4 servings.

with 1/3 cup almonds and calculated without rice) equals 331 calories, 15 g fat (2 g saturated fat), 66 mg cholesterol, 843 mg sodium, 19 g carbohydrate, 5 g fiber, 29 g protein. **Diabetic Exchanges:** 3-1/2 lean meat, 1 starch, 1 vegetable, 1 fat.

Almond Chicken Stir-Fry

(Pictured above)

Denise Uhlenhake, Ossian, Iowa

Almonds and water chestnuts add crunch to this speedy supper. It's great with frozen stir-fry vegetables, too.

✓ Uses less fat, sugar or salt. Includes Nutritional Analysis and Diabetic Exchanges.

1-1/2 **pounds boneless skinless chicken breasts, cut into strips**
   3 **tablespoons canola oil**
1-1/2 **cups cauliflowerets**
1-1/2 **cups broccoli florets**
  3/4 **cup julienned carrots**
  1/2 **cup chopped celery**
  1/4 **cup chopped sweet red pepper**
   1 **can (8 ounces) sliced water chestnuts, drained**
   3 **cups chicken broth**
   3 **tablespoons reduced-sodium soy sauce**
  1/3 **cup cornstarch**
  1/2 **cup cold water**
Hot cooked rice, optional
  1/3 **to 1/2 cup slivered almonds, toasted**

In a skillet or wok, stir-fry chicken in oil until no longer pink. Stir in the cauliflower, broccoli, carrots, celery, red pepper, water chestnuts, broth and soy sauce. Bring to a boil. Reduce heat to low; cover and cook until vegetables are crisp-tender.

Combine the cornstarch and water until smooth; stir into chicken mixture. Bring to a boil; cook and stir for 2 minutes or until thickened. Serve stir-fry over rice if desired. Sprinkle with almonds. **Yield:** 6 servings.

Nutritional Analysis: One 1-cup serving (prepared

Spicy Chicken Linguine

Tracy Haroldson, Aztec, New Mexico

Our state is famous for its green chilies. Naturally, my husband and I included them in this linguine dish we invented. It is also excellent with spaghetti or fettuccine.

  1/4 **cup butter**
   3 **tablespoons all-purpose flour**
   2 **teaspoons garlic powder**
   1 **teaspoon pepper**
2-1/2 **cups milk**
   1 **package (8 ounces) cream cheese, cubed**
   1 **cup (4 ounces) shredded Parmesan cheese**
  12 **ounces uncooked linguine**
   3 **cups cubed cooked chicken**
   1 **can (4 ounces) diced green chilies**

In a saucepan, melt butter. Stir in the flour, garlic powder and pepper until smooth. Gradually add the milk. Bring to a boil; cook and stir for 2 minutes or until thickened. Reduce heat; add cream cheese and Parmesan cheese. Cook and stir for 8-10 minutes or until the cheese is melted.

Meanwhile, cook linguine according to package directions. Add chicken and chilies to cheese sauce; cook 5 minutes longer or until heated through. Drain linguine; top with chicken mixture. **Yield:** 6 servings.

Ginger Peach Chicken

Patty Gale, Pepperell, Massachusetts

My family is always glad to see this hearty skillet dinner on busy nights. It goes together quickly with ingredients that I keep on hand. I often serve it with a side of rice or pasta.

   1 **can (16 ounces) sliced peaches**
   4 **boneless skinless chicken breast halves (4 ounces *each*)**
   1 **tablespoon butter**
   1 **tablespoon cornstarch**
  1/2 **teaspoon salt**
   1 **teaspoon minced fresh gingerroot**
   1 **can (8 ounces) sliced water chestnuts, drained**

Drain peaches, reserving juice; set peaches aside. Add water to juice to measure 3/4 cup. Flatten chicken breasts to 1/2-in. thickness. In a nonstick skillet, cook chicken in butter over medium heat for 5-6 minutes on each side or until juices run clear. Remove and keep warm.

In a bowl, combine cornstarch, peach liquid, salt and ginger until smooth; stir into skillet. Bring to a boil; cook and stir for 2 minutes or until thickened. Add peaches and water chestnuts; heat through. Spoon over chicken. **Yield:** 4 servings.

Bow Tie Chicken Supper

(Pictured below)

Nancy Daugherty, Cortland, Ohio

My sister-in-law gave me a recipe for a healthy side dish, and I added chicken to it to make this colorful main course. It's wonderful with a salad and crusty bread. I love the chicken mixed wih sweet red pepper, zucchini, peas and tomatoes!

✓ Uses less fat, sugar or salt. Includes Nutritional Analysis and Diabetic Exchanges.

1 pound boneless skinless chicken breasts, cut into 1/4-inch strips
1 tablespoon canola oil
1 small sweet red pepper, julienned
1 small zucchini, cut into 1/4-inch slices
1 small onion, chopped
2 garlic cloves, minced
1/2 cup frozen peas, thawed
1 teaspoon Italian seasoning
1/4 teaspoon salt-free seasoning blend
1 cup bow tie pasta, cooked and drained
2 medium tomatoes, seeded and chopped
1/4 cup shredded Parmesan cheese

In a large nonstick skillet, saute chicken in oil for 3-5 minutes or until juices run clear. Remove and keep warm. In the same skillet, stir-fry red pepper, zucchini, onion and garlic for 3-4 minutes or until vegetables are crisp-tender.

Add the peas and seasonings; stir-fry for 2 minutes. Add pasta and tomatoes; cook for 1 minute. Remove from the heat. Gently stir in chicken. Sprinkle with cheese. **Yield:** 4 servings.

Nutritional Analysis: One serving (1-1/2 cups) equals 256 calories, 7 g fat (2 g saturated fat), 71 mg cholesterol, 219 mg sodium, 15 g carbohydrate, 3 g fiber, 32 g protein. **Diabetic Exchanges:** 3 lean meat, 1 starch.

Creole Skillet Dinner

(Pictured below)

Bonnie Brann, Pasco, Washington

While living in Canada, I sampled this colorful dish at a neighbor's. The following Christmas, I served it instead of my traditional turkey, and I received numerous compliments on it.

       4 cups chicken broth
2-1/2 cups uncooked long grain rice
       1 cup chopped red onion
       3 garlic cloves, minced, *divided*
1-1/4 teaspoons chili powder
       1 teaspoon salt
     1/2 teaspoon ground turmeric
     1/4 teaspoon pepper
       1 bay leaf
       1 sweet red pepper, julienned
       1 green pepper, julienned
       2 green onions, sliced
       1 teaspoon chopped fresh parsley
     1/2 teaspoon dried basil
     1/2 teaspoon dried thyme
     1/4 teaspoon hot pepper sauce
       2 tablespoons butter
       1 cup sliced fresh mushrooms
       1 medium tomato, chopped
       1 cup frozen peas
       1 pound boneless skinless chicken breasts, thinly sliced
       2 tablespoons lemon juice
     1/3 cup sliced almonds, toasted

In a saucepan, bring broth, rice, onion, 1 teaspoon garlic, chili powder, salt, turmeric, pepper and bay leaf to

a boil. Reduce heat; cover and simmer 20 minutes or until rice is tender. Discard bay leaf.

In a skillet over medium-high heat, saute the next seven ingredients and remaining garlic in butter for 2 minutes. Add mushrooms; cook until peppers are crisp-tender. Add tomato and peas; heat through. Remove from the heat.

Add rice; keep warm. Over medium-high heat, cook and stir chicken in lemon juice until chicken juices run clear. Add to rice mixture; toss. Top with almonds. **Yield:** 6-8 servings.

Pasta, Chicken and Squash

(Pictured above)

Pam Hall, Elizabeth City, North Carolina

This is a special dish that we enjoy often. The combination of chicken, pasta and squash is so pleasing. It's a skillet supper that's delicious and pretty, too.

       1 package (16 ounces) spiral pasta
       2 cups heavy whipping cream
       1 tablespoon butter
       2 cups (8 ounces) shredded Mexican cheese blend
       1 small onion, chopped
       1 garlic clove, minced
       5 tablespoons olive oil, *divided*
       2 medium zucchini, julienned
       2 medium yellow summer squash, julienned
1-1/4 teaspoons salt, *divided*
     1/8 teaspoon pepper

1 pound boneless skinless chicken breasts,
  julienned
1/4 teaspoon *each* dried basil, marjoram
  and savory
1/4 teaspoon dried rosemary, crushed
1/8 teaspoon rubbed sage

Cook pasta according to package directions. Meanwhile, heat cream and butter in a large saucepan until butter melts. Add cheese; cook and stir until melted. Rinse and drain pasta; add to cheese mixture. Cover and keep warm.

In a skillet over medium heat, saute onion and garlic in 3 tablespoons oil until onion is tender. Add zucchini and squash; cook until tender. Add 1 teaspoon of salt and pepper; remove and keep warm. Add remaining oil to skillet; cook chicken with herbs and remaining salt until juices run clear. Place pasta on a serving platter; top with chicken and squash. **Yield:** 8 servings.

Chicken a la King

Polly Hurst, Flemingsburg, Kentucky

Thanks to the especially easy preparation, this recipe is guaranteed to get the cook out of the kitchen—and on to enjoying the day—extra quickly.

1/4 cup butter
1/3 cup all-purpose flour
1/2 teaspoon salt
  1 cup chicken broth
  1 cup milk
  2 cups diced cooked chicken
  1 can (4 ounces) mushroom stems and pieces,
    drained
  1 jar (2 ounces) diced pimientos, drained
Toast points

In a saucepan, melt the butter; stir in the flour and salt until smooth. Add the broth and milk; bring to a boil over medium heat. Cook and stir for 2 minutes or until thickened.

Stir in the chicken, mushrooms and pimientos; heat through. Serve over the toast points. **Yield:** 4 servings.

Tropical Chicken

(Pictured below left)

Leah Johnson, Pearl City, Hawaii

We enjoy the way the sweetness of the pineapple balances the garlic and hot pepper in this hearty colorful dish. We make this often since my husband and I live only minutes from pineapple fields.

  1 broiler/fryer chicken (3-1/2 to 4 pounds),
    cut up
  3 tablespoons vegetable oil, *divided*
3/4 cup chopped onion
  2 garlic cloves, minced
  3 medium tomatoes, peeled and chopped
  3 cups fresh *or* canned pineapple chunks
1/4 cup pineapple juice
  1 hot red pepper (4-1/2 to 5 inches), seeded
    and chopped
3/4 teaspoon salt
1/4 teaspoon pepper
  1 can (8 ounces) sliced water chestnuts,
    drained
1/2 pound fresh snow peas
  1 tablespoon chopped fresh chives
Hot cooked rice

In a skillet over medium heat, brown the chicken in 2 tablespoons of oil; remove and set aside. In the same skillet, saute the onion and garlic in remaining oil until tender. Add tomatoes, pineapple, pineapple juice, red pepper, salt, pepper and water chestnuts.

Return chicken to the pan; bring to a boil. Reduce heat; cover and simmer for 45 minutes. Add peas and chives; cover and simmer for 10-15 minutes or until peas are tender and chicken juices run clear. Thicken the pan juices if desired. Serve over rice. **Yield:** 6 servings.

Editor's Note: When cutting or seeding hot peppers, use rubber or plastic gloves to protect your hands. Avoid touching your face.

Chicken in Creamy Gravy

(Pictured below)

Jean Little, Charlotte, North Carolina

You only need a few ingredients and a few minutes to put this tasty main dish on the table. A burst of lemon in every bite makes it a well-received standby.

✓ Uses less fat, sugar or salt. Includes Nutritional Analysis and Diabetic Exchanges.

 4 boneless skinless chicken breast halves
   (1 pound)
 1 tablespoon canola oil
 1 can (10-3/4 ounces) reduced-fat reduced-sodium condensed cream of chicken and broccoli soup, undiluted
 1/4 cup fat-free milk
 2 teaspoons lemon juice
 1/8 teaspoon pepper
 4 lemon slices
Hot cooked linguine, optional

In a nonstick skillet, cook chicken in oil until browned on both sides, about 10 minutes; drain. In a bowl, combine soup, milk, lemon juice and pepper. Pour over chicken. Top each chicken breast with a lemon slice. Reduce heat; cover and simmer until chicken juices run clear, about 5 minutes. Serve with linguine if desired. **Yield:** 4 servings.

Nutritional Analysis: One serving (calculated without linguine) equals 232 calories, 7 g fat (1 g saturated fat), 72 mg cholesterol, 644 mg sodium, 18 g carbohydrate, 5 g fiber, 30 g protein. **Diabetic Exchanges:** 3 lean meat, 1 starch.

Apricot Salsa Chicken

Grace Yaskovic, Branchville, New Jersey

In an unusual but tongue-tingling combination, apricots and salsa smother pieces of chicken with a sweet and spicy sauce to make this tasty recipe. People often ask for the recipe and are surprised at how easy it is to make!

 1/2 cup all-purpose flour
   1 teaspoon salt
 1/4 teaspoon pepper
 1/4 teaspoon paprika

    6 boneless skinless chicken breast halves
       (about 1-1/2 pounds)
    3 tablespoons vegetable oil
    1 jar (16 ounces) salsa
    1 jar (12 ounces) apricot preserves
 1/2 cup apricot nectar
Hot cooked rice

In a shallow bowl, combine the flour, salt, pepper and paprika. Add chicken; turn to coat. In a skillet, brown chicken in oil; drain. Stir in salsa, preserves and nectar; bring to a boil.

Reduce heat; simmer, uncovered, for 15 minutes or until sauce thickens and meat juices run clear. Serve over rice. **Yield:** 6 servings.

Chicken Stir-Fry

(Pictured at right)

Lori Schlecht, Wimbledon, North Dakota

This is a tasty, healthy meal that everyone in my house enjoys! You can mix up the selection of veggies to use your favorites, but we like using broccoli, celery, carrots and onions.

✓ Uses less fat, sugar or salt. Includes Nutritional Analysis and Diabetic Exchanges.

    4 boneless skinless chicken breast halves
       (1 pound)
    3 tablespoons cornstarch
    2 tablespoons reduced-fat soy sauce
 1/2 teaspoon ground ginger
 1/4 teaspoon garlic powder
    3 tablespoons vegetable oil, *divided*
    2 cups broccoli florets
    1 cup sliced celery (1/2-inch pieces)
    1 cup thinly sliced carrots
    1 small onion, cut into wedges
    1 cup water
    1 teaspoon reduced-sodium chicken bouillon
       granules

Cut chicken into 1/2-in. strips; place in a resealable plastic bag. Add cornstarch and toss to coat. Combine soy sauce, ginger and garlic powder; add to bag and shake well. Refrigerate for 30 minutes.

In a large skillet or wok, heat 2 tablespoons of oil; stir-fry chicken until no longer pink, about 3-5 minutes. Remove and keep warm.

Add remaining oil; stir-fry broccoli, celery, carrots and onion for 4-5 minutes or until crisp-tender. Add water and bouillon. Return chicken to pan. Cook and stir until thickened and bubbly. **Yield:** 4 servings.

Nutritional Analysis: One serving equals 306 calories, 239 mg sodium, 73 mg cholesterol, 18 g carbohydrate, 30 g protein, 14 g fat. **Diabetic Exchanges:** 3 lean meat, 2 vegetable, 1 fat, 1/2 starch.

Raspberry Thyme Chicken

Lenita Schafer, Princeton, Massachusetts

Here's an easy way to dress up chicken. I guarantee you won't miss the fat and calories when you taste this tender poultry with berry sauce.

✓ Uses less fat, sugar or salt. Includes Nutritional Analysis and Diabetic Exchanges.

 1/2 cup chopped red onion
    2 teaspoons canola oil
1-1/2 teaspoons minced fresh thyme *or* 1/2
       teaspoon dried thyme
 1/2 teaspoon salt, *divided*
    4 boneless skinless chicken breast halves
       (1 pound)
 1/3 cup seedless raspberry preserves
    2 tablespoons balsamic vinegar
 1/8 teaspoon pepper

In a nonstick skillet, saute onion in oil until tender. Sprinkle thyme and 1/4 teaspoon salt over chicken; add to skillet. Cook for 5 minutes on each side or until juices run clear. Remove chicken and keep warm.

Add the preserves, vinegar, pepper and remaining salt to skillet. Cook and stir over medium-low heat until preserves are melted and sauce is heated through. Spoon onto a serving platter; top with chicken. **Yield:** 4 servings.

Nutritional Analysis: One serving (1 chicken breast half with 2 tablespoons sauce) equals 227 calories, 4 g fat (1 g saturated fat), 66 mg cholesterol, 383 mg sodium, 21 g carbohydrate, trace fiber, 27 g protein. **Diabetic Exchanges:** 3 lean meat, 1 starch.

Chicken Fajitas

(Pictured above)

Julie Sterchi, Harrisburg, Illinois

The marinated chicken in these popular wraps is mouth-watering. They go together in a snap and always get raves!

    4 tablespoons vegetable oil, *divided*
    2 tablespoons lemon juice
1-1/2 teaspoons seasoned salt
1-1/2 teaspoons dried oregano
1-1/2 teaspoons ground cumin
    1 teaspoon garlic powder
  1/2 teaspoon chili powder
  1/2 teaspoon paprika
  1/2 teaspoon crushed red pepper flakes,
        optional
1-1/2 pounds boneless skinless chicken breasts,
        cut into thin strips
  1/2 medium sweet red pepper, julienned
  1/2 medium green pepper, julienned
    4 green onions, thinly sliced
  1/2 cup chopped onion
    6 flour tortillas (8 inches), warmed
Shredded cheddar cheese, taco sauce, salsa,
    guacamole *and/or* sour cream

In a large resealable plastic bag, combine 2 tablespoons oil, lemon juice and seasonings. Add chicken. Seal and turn to coat; refrigerate for 1-4 hours.

In a large skillet, saute peppers and onions in remaining oil until crisp-tender. Remove and keep warm. In the same skillet, cook chicken and marinade over medium-high heat for 5-6 minutes or until the chicken is no longer pink.

Return pepper mixture to pan; heat through. Spoon filling down the center of tortillas; fold in half. Serve with cheddar cheese, taco sauce, salsa, guacamole and/or sour cream. **Yield:** 6 servings.

Pesto Mushroom Chicken

Jennifer Tomlinson, Hamilton, Montana

My husband is an avid hunter, so we enjoy lots of game. But when I cook chicken, this is the recipe I turn to. Pesto, cheese and mushrooms make it flavorful and special.

    4 boneless skinless chicken breast halves
Salt and pepper to taste
    5 tablespoons olive oil, *divided*
    1 cup loosely packed fresh basil leaves
  1/2 cup chopped walnuts
    2 garlic cloves, minced
  1/2 teaspoon salt
  1/3 cup grated Parmesan cheese

4 slices mozzarella cheese
1 cup sliced fresh mushrooms

Flatten chicken to 1/4-in. thickness; sprinkle with salt and pepper. In a large skillet, cook chicken in 1 tablespoon oil for 5-10 minutes on each side or until juices run clear.

Meanwhile, for pesto, combine the basil, nuts, garlic, salt and Parmesan cheese in a blender or food processor; cover and process until well blended. While processing, gradually add remaining oil in a stream.

Spoon over chicken. Top each with a slice of mozzarella. Sprinkle mushrooms around chicken. Cover and cook for 5 minutes or until cheese is melted and mushrooms are tender. **Yield:** 4 servings.

Tangy Pineapple Chicken

(Pictured below)

Jean Ecos, Waukesha, Wisconsin

Tender chicken in a tangy sauce is topped with pretty pineapple to make a mouth-watering main dish.

✓ Uses less fat, sugar or salt. Includes Nutritional Analysis and Diabetic Exchanges.

4 boneless skinless chicken breast halves
  (1 pound)
1 teaspoon dried thyme
1/2 teaspoon salt
1/8 teaspoon pepper
1 tablespoon vegetable oil
1 can (20 ounces) unsweetened sliced
  pineapple

1 tablespoon cornstarch
1/4 cup Dijon mustard
1/4 cup honey
2 garlic cloves, minced
Hot cooked rice

Sprinkle chicken with thyme, salt and pepper. In a skillet, brown chicken in oil. Meanwhile, drain pineapple, reserving the juice. Cut pineapple rings in half and set aside.

Combine cornstarch and 2 tablespoons juice until smooth; set aside. Combine mustard, honey, garlic and remaining pineapple juice; mix well. Add to pan; bring to a boil. Reduce heat; cover and simmer for 15-20 minutes or until chicken juices run clear.

Remove the chicken and keep warm. Stir the cornstarch mixture and add to pan; bring to a boil. Boil and stir for 2 minutes. Return the chicken to pan. Top with the pineapple; heat through. Serve over rice. **Yield:** 4 servings.

Nutritional Analysis: One serving (calculated without rice) equals 351 calories, 736 mg sodium, 73 mg cholesterol, 44 g carbohydrate, 28 g protein, 8 g fat. **Diabetic Exchanges:** 4 very lean meat, 3 fruit, 1/2 fat.

Chicken in Pear Sauce

Andrea Lunsford, Spokane, Washington

Pairing poultry with pears brought applause from my husband and four growing children. Simple enough for everyday meals and ideal for company, this dish is a year-round standout. We enjoy it with boiled potatoes.

4 boneless skinless chicken breast halves
1/2 teaspoon salt
1/8 teaspoon white pepper
2 tablespoons vegetable oil
5 thick-cut bacon strips, diced
1 can (14-1/2 ounces) chicken broth
2 to 3 medium ripe pears, peeled and diced
2 tablespoons cornstarch
2 tablespoons cold water
1/4 cup snipped chives

Sprinkle chicken with salt and pepper. In a skillet over medium heat, cook chicken in oil on both sides for about 10 minutes or until juices run clear.

Meanwhile, in a saucepan, cook bacon until crisp. Drain, reserving 1 tablespoon drippings; set bacon aside. Gradually stir broth into the drippings, scraping pan to loosen browned bits. Bring to a boil. Boil, uncovered, for 5 minutes. Add pears; return to a boil. Boil, uncovered, for 5 minutes or until pears are tender.

Combine cornstarch and water until smooth; add the chives. Gradually stir into pear sauce; bring to a boil. Cook and stir for 2 minutes or until thickened and bubbly. Stir in bacon. Serve over the chicken. **Yield:** 4 servings.

Peanutty Chicken

(Pictured below)

Mary Kay Dixson, Decatur, Alabama

Peanuts are great in both sweet and savory recipes; one delicious main dish is this tender chicken. Covered in a tasty gravy and sprinkled with peanuts, it has a zip that perks up taste buds.

- 1 teaspoon chili powder
- 1 teaspoon salt
- 1/4 teaspoon pepper
- 1 broiler/fryer chicken (3-1/2 to 4 pounds), cut up
- 5 tablespoons butter
- 1 cup orange juice
- 2/3 to 1 cup salted peanuts

Orange slices and minced fresh cilantro, optional

Combine chili powder, salt and pepper; rub over chicken. In a large skillet, saute chicken in butter until golden brown. Reduce heat; cover and cook until juices run clear, about 30 minutes. Transfer chicken to a serving platter and keep warm.

Add orange juice to skillet, stirring to loosen browned bits from pan; simmer for 5 minutes. Pour over chicken. Sprinkle with peanuts. Garnish with orange slices and cilantro if desired. **Yield:** 4 servings.

Basil Cream Chicken

Billie Vaughan, Slinger, Wisconsin

I love to sprinkle basil over chicken, meats, pasta and egg dishes. It also stars in this recipe, which features a creamy sauce for the chicken.

- 1-1/2 pounds boneless skinless chicken breasts, cubed
- 1-1/3 cups finely chopped green onions
- 1 pound fresh mushrooms, sliced
- 2 tablespoons vegetable oil
- 1/2 cup butter
- 1/4 cup all-purpose flour
- 2 cups chicken broth
- 1 cup heavy whipping cream
- 2 tablespoons minced fresh basil *or* 2 teaspoons dried basil
- 1/4 teaspoon white pepper

Hot cooked fettuccine

In a skillet, saute chicken, onions and mushrooms in oil until the chicken is no longer pink. Meanwhile, in a large saucepan, melt butter. Stir in flour until smooth.

Gradually add the broth and cream. Stir in the basil and pepper. Bring to a boil; cook and stir for 2 minutes or until thickened. Stir in chicken mixture. Serve over fettuccine. **Yield:** 6-8 servings.

Chicken Vinaigrette

Jean Pare, Vermilion, Alberta

My motto is "never share a recipe you wouldn't use yourself." This is one I use often because it has a tasty mix of chicken and vegetables.

- 1 broiler/fryer chicken (3 pounds), cut up and skin removed
- 1 teaspoon vegetable oil

Salt and pepper to taste
- 1 large onion, chopped
- 1 garlic clove, minced
- 4 medium carrots, sliced
- 4 medium red potatoes, halved
- 1/2 cup water
- 1 tablespoon minced fresh parsley
- 1 teaspoon dried basil
- 1/2 teaspoon chicken bouillon granules

Pinch dried thyme
- 1/2 cup *each* chopped sweet red and yellow pepper (1-inch pieces)
- 2 green onions, sliced
- 1/4 cup red wine vinegar

In a nonstick skillet, brown chicken in oil. Sprinkle with salt and pepper. Remove and keep warm. In drippings, saute onion and garlic until tender. Stir in carrots, potatoes, water and seasonings; top with chicken.

Reduce heat; cover and simmer for 25 minutes, stirring occasionally. Stir in additional water if needed. Add peppers and green onions.

Cover and cook until chicken juices run clear and vegetables are tender, about 5 minutes. Stir in vinegar; heat through. **Yield:** 4 servings.

Crispy Chicken Cutlets

Debra Smith, Brookfield, Missouri

These cutlets are moist and tender with a golden nutty coating. This is an easy entree I proudly serve to company. Everyone raves about the crunchy coating, and I always get recipe requests.

- 4 boneless skinless chicken breast halves
- 1 egg white
- 3/4 cup finely chopped pecans
- 3 tablespoons all-purpose flour
- 1/4 teaspoon salt
- 1/4 teaspoon pepper
- 1 tablespoon butter
- 1 tablespoon vegetable oil

Flatten chicken to 1/4-in. thickness. In a shallow bowl, lightly beat egg white. In another shallow bowl, combine pecans, flour, salt and pepper. Dip chicken in egg white, then coat with pecan mixture.

In a large skillet, brown chicken in butter and oil over

medium heat for 4-6 minutes on each side or until juices run clear. **Yield:** 4 servings.

Orange Onion Chicken

(Pictured above)

Alcy Thorne, Los Molinos, California

The combination of chicken, seasonings and oranges makes a satisfying meal. This is one of my family's favorite dishes.

- 4 boneless skinless chicken breast halves (1-1/4 pounds)
- 2 tablespoons vegetable oil
- 1-1/4 cups water, *divided*
- 1/2 cup orange juice
- 1/4 cup chopped onion
- 1/4 cup chicken broth
- 1/4 to 1/2 teaspoon ground ginger
- 2 tablespoons cornstarch
- 2 oranges, peeled and sectioned

In a skillet, brown chicken in oil; drain. Add 1 cup water, orange juice, onion, broth and ginger. Cover and simmer until chicken juices run clear, 20-25 minutes. Remove chicken; keep warm.

Mix cornstarch with remaining water; stir into skillet. Cook and stir until thickened and bubbly; cook and stir for 2 minutes more. Add orange sections and heat through. Serve over chicken. **Yield:** 4 servings.

Chicken Stroganoff

(Pictured below)

Laura Schimanski, Coaldale, Alberta

I came up with this recipe, a variation on beef Stroganoff, as a way to use up roasted chicken. It was a hit. I'm usually the only one in my family who enjoys noodles, but even our son will have more when they're topped with this creamy chicken.

- 4 bacon strips, diced
- 1 pound boneless skinless chicken breasts, cut into 1/4-inch strips
- 1 medium onion, chopped
- 2 jars (4-1/2 ounces *each*) sliced mushrooms, drained
- 1-1/2 cups chicken broth
- 2 garlic cloves, minced
- 1/2 teaspoon salt
- 1/8 teaspoon paprika
- Pepper to taste
- 2 tablespoons all-purpose flour
- 1 cup (8 ounces) sour cream
- Hot cooked noodles
- Additional paprika, optional

In a skillet, cook bacon until crisp. Drain, reserving 2 tablespoons drippings; set bacon aside. In the drippings, cook the chicken, onion and mushrooms until the chicken juices run clear. Add the broth, garlic, salt, paprika, pepper and bacon. Cover and simmer for 10 minutes.

Combine flour and sour cream until smooth; add to the skillet. Bring to a boil; cook and stir for 2 minutes

or until thickened. Serve over noodles. Sprinkle with paprika if desired. **Yield:** 4 servings.

Chicken Wings Fricassee

(Pictured above)

Sundra Lewis, Bogalusa, Louisiana

This comforting, old-fashioned dish with flavorful gravy uses inexpensive chicken wings for an impressive dinner. It usually prompts compliments—and second helpings.

- 12 whole chicken wings (about 2-1/2 pounds)
- 1/3 to 1/2 cup all-purpose flour
- 1 teaspoon seasoned salt
- 3/4 teaspoon pepper, *divided*
- 3 tablespoons vegetable oil
- 2 medium onions, chopped
- 1 garlic clove, minced
- 1-1/4 cups water
- 1 teaspoon salt
- Hot cooked rice

Cut chicken wings into three sections; discard wing tips. In a resealable plastic bag or shallow bowl, combine flour, seasoned salt and 1/2 teaspoon pepper. Add wings; toss to coat evenly.

In a large skillet, brown wings on all sides in oil. Add onions and garlic; cook until tender. Stir in the water, salt and remaining pepper; mix well. Bring to a boil; reduce heat.

Simmer, uncovered, for 30-35 minutes or until chicken juices run clear. Serve over rice. **Yield:** 4 servings.

Editor's Note: 2-1/2 pounds of uncooked chicken wing sections (wingettes) may be substituted for the whole chicken wings. Omit the first step of recipe.

Chicken with Blueberry Sauce

Thomas Jewell Sr., Avenel, New Jersey

Blueberries mix with apricot jam and mustard to create a sweet and tangy sauce for this tender chicken. The fruit sauce makes this dish extra special.

☑ Uses less fat, sugar or salt. Includes Nutritional Analysis and Diabetic Exchanges.

    4 boneless skinless chicken breast halves
      (1 pound)
    1 tablespoon vegetable oil
  1/2 cup 100% apricot fruit spread
    3 tablespoons Dijon mustard
  1/3 cup white wine vinegar
  1/2 cup fresh *or* frozen blueberries
Hot cooked rice, optional

In a large skillet over medium heat, cook chicken in oil for about 4 minutes on each side or until lightly browned. Combine preserves and mustard; spoon over chicken. Reduce heat; cover and simmer for 15 minutes or until chicken juices run clear.

With a slotted spoon, remove chicken and keep warm. Add vinegar to skillet; bring to a boil. Reduce heat; simmer, uncovered, for 3 minutes or until sauce is reduced by one-third, stirring occasionally. Stir in blueberries and heat through. Serve over chicken and rice if desired. **Yield:** 4 servings.
Nutritional Analysis: One serving (calculated without rice) equals 264 calories, 6 g fat (1 g saturated fat), 66 mg cholesterol, 360 mg sodium, 26 g carbohydrate, 1 g fiber, 27 g protein. **Diabetic Exchanges:** 3 lean meat, 1-1/2 fruit.

Chicken with Cucumbers

(Pictured at right)

Angela Avedon, Mooresville, North Carolina

This interesting chicken dish gets a fresh flavor from the cucumbers. I like to entertain family and friends, and I collect cookbooks. This recipe came from one of my many books and is well received by whoever tries it.

Cucumbers Make the Cut

Cucumbers should be used within 4 or 5 days of purchase. If a cucumber tastes bitter, cut off the stem ends and peel. To use up a bounty of cucumbers, add sliced cucumbers to tossed salads or mix shredded cucumbers with dill and sour cream for a tasty dip.

    1 broiler/fryer chicken (3-1/2 to 4 pounds),
      cut up
    2 tablespoons vegetable oil
  1/4 pound fresh mushrooms, sliced
    1 garlic clove, minced
    3 tablespoons all-purpose flour
1-3/4 cups water
    1 tablespoon chicken bouillon granules
    2 large cucumbers
    1 cup (8 ounces) sour cream

In a large skillet over medium heat, brown chicken in oil. Remove chicken; set aside. To drippings, add mushrooms and garlic; saute 2 minutes. Stir in flour until the mushrooms are coated. Gradually add water and bouillon; cook and stir over medium heat until bubbly.

Return chicken to the skillet; bring to a boil. Reduce the heat; cover and simmer for 30 minutes, stirring occasionally.

Meanwhile, thinly slice one cucumber and set the slices aside. Peel remaining cucumber; slice in half lengthwise and remove seeds. Cut into 1-in. chunks. Add to skillet and simmer for 20 minutes or until chicken juices run clear. Stir sour cream into sauce; heat through but do not boil. Garnish with reserved cucumber slices. **Yield:** 4-6 servings.

3 Grilled Dishes

Glazed Herb Chicken

(Pictured at left)

Jill Smith, Irmo, South Carolina

The orange flavor really comes through in the sauce that nicely coats this grilled chicken. I like to garnish it with fresh orange segments and a sprinkling of green chives for a pretty look. Guests will rave over this delightful dish!

✓ Uses less fat, sugar or salt. Includes Nutritional Analysis and Diabetic Exchanges.

  1 can (14-1/2 ounces) chicken broth
3/4 cup orange juice concentrate
  2 tablespoons red wine vinegar
  2 teaspoons grated orange peel
  2 garlic cloves, minced
1/2 teaspoon dried minced onion
1/8 to 1/4 teaspoon cayenne pepper
1/8 teaspoon dried thyme
1/8 teaspoon ground allspice
  4 boneless skinless chicken breast halves
    (1 pound)
  1 tablespoon cornstarch
1/4 cup honey
  1 medium navel orange, peeled and sectioned
  3 cups hot cooked rice
  2 teaspoons minced chives

In a bowl, combine the chicken broth, orange juice concentrate, vinegar, orange peel, garlic, minced onion, cayenne, thyme and allspice. Remove 1 cup for sauce; cover and refrigerate.

Place the chicken in a large resealable plastic bag; add the remaining marinade. Seal bag and turn to coat; refrigerate for 2-8 hours, turning occasionally. Drain and discard marinade. Grill chicken, uncovered, over medium heat for 4 minutes on each side or until the chicken juices run clear.

Meanwhile, in a saucepan, combine the cornstarch and reserved marinade until smooth. Stir in the honey. Bring to a boil; cook and stir for 2 minutes or until thickened. Serve chicken with orange sections over rice; spoon sauce over top. Sprinkle with chives. **Yield:** 4 servings.

Nutritional Analysis: One serving (1 chicken breast half with 1/4 cup sauce) equals 276 calories, 2 g fat (1 g saturated fat), 66 mg cholesterol, 912 mg sodium, 37 g carbohydrate, 2 g fiber, 28 g protein. **Diabetic Exchanges:** 3 lean meat, 1-1/2 starch.

Grilled Chicken Salad

Dawn Davidson, Thornton, Ontario

This tasty salad is fast to assemble, and cleanup's a breeze. Serve it with the warmed dressing and crusty bread, and you have a meal that the whole family is sure to love.

1/4 cup olive oil
1/4 cup chicken broth
  3 tablespoons lemon juice
  1 teaspoon dried basil
  1 teaspoon dried oregano
  1 teaspoon Dijon mustard
1/4 teaspoon salt
1/4 teaspoon lemon-pepper seasoning
  4 boneless skinless chicken breast halves
  1 large red onion, sliced and separated into rings
10 cups torn romaine
  1 medium sweet red pepper, chopped
3/4 cup crumbled feta cheese

In a bowl, combine the first eight ingredients; mix well. Place half in a saucepan and set aside. Brush remaining vinaigrette over chicken and onion rings. Grill chicken and onion, covered, over medium heat for 12 minutes or until meat juices run clear, turning once. Cut chicken into 1/2-in. slices.

In a large bowl or on salad plates, layer romaine, onion, chicken, red pepper and cheese. Heat the reserved vinaigrette; drizzle over salad. Serve immediately. **Yield:** 8 servings.

Grilling Chicken

Before starting the grill, coat the grill rack with non-stick cooking spray. It will help prevent your chicken from sticking and make it easier to turn.

Cook boneless chicken breast halves to an internal temperature of 170°; bone-in chicken parts should reach 170° for white meat and 180° for dark meat.

Lemon-Garlic Grilled Chicken

Donna Leuw, Calgary, Alberta

This tasty recipe is used often during summer; we can hardly wait until grilling season begins!

- 4 boneless skinless chicken breast halves (1 pound)
- 2 tablespoons lemon juice
- 2 teaspoons olive oil
- 1 garlic clove, minced
- 1/2 teaspoon dried oregano
- 1/8 teaspoon cayenne pepper

Place chicken in a resealable plastic bag or shallow glass container. Combine remaining ingredients; pour over chicken. Seal bag or cover container. Refrigerate 20 minutes, turning once. Drain and discard marinade.

Grill chicken, uncovered, over medium-hot heat for 12-15 minutes or until the juices run clear, turning once. **Yield:** 4 servings.

Lemon Barbecued Chicken

(Pictured above)

Rondella Brown, Hanover, Pennsylvania

My husband loves chicken, so when we bought our first charcoal grill, we needed a recipe for barbecued chicken. We ended up combining two of the best recipes we found to come up with this one that features the refreshing citrus flavor of lemon juice.

- 2/3 cup lemon juice
- 1/3 cup vegetable oil
- 1/3 cup vinegar
- 1 tablespoon soy sauce
- 2 teaspoons sugar
- 1 teaspoon salt
- 1 teaspoon paprika
- 1 teaspoon chili powder
- 1/2 teaspoon pepper
- 1/2 teaspoon garlic salt
- 1 medium onion, chopped
- 1 broiler/fryer chicken (3-1/2 to 4 pounds), cut up

Whisk together the lemon juice, oil, vinegar, soy sauce, sugar, salt, paprika, chili powder, pepper, garlic salt and chopped onion; set aside 1/4 cup of marinade.

Pour the remaining marinade into a large resealable plastic bag. Add chicken; seal bag. Refrigerate at least 8 hours or overnight, turning occasionally. Drain, discarding marinade.

Grill chicken, covered, over medium heat for 45 minutes or until chicken juices run clear, turning and basting with reserved marinade every 8-10 minutes.

To bake chicken: After marinating, place chicken in a greased 15-in. x 10-in. x 1-in. baking pan. Pour all of the marinade over it. Bake, uncovered, at 350° for 1-1/4 hours or until juices run clear, basting occasionally. **Yield:** 6 servings.

Luau Chicken Sandwiches

(Pictured below)

Denise Pope, Mishawaka, Indiana

A friend at work gave me the recipe for this marinade. After grilling the tender chicken a few times for company, I decided to turn it into a sandwich.

- 1 can (20 ounces) sliced pineapple
- 1 tablespoon brown sugar
- 1 teaspoon ground mustard
- 1 teaspoon garlic salt
- 1/2 teaspoon pepper
- 6 boneless skinless chicken breast halves

1/4 cup mayonnaise
1 tablespoon Dijon mustard
1/4 teaspoon dill weed
6 kaiser rolls, split and toasted
6 lettuce leaves, optional

Drain pineapple, reserving 1 cup juice and six pineapple slices (save remaining juice and pineapple for another use). In a large resealable plastic bag, combine the brown sugar, ground mustard, garlic salt, pepper and reserved pineapple juice; add chicken. Seal bag and turn to coat; refrigerate for at least 2 hours, turning occasionally. In a small bowl, combine the mayonnaise, Dijon mustard and dill. Refrigerate until serving.

Drain and discard marinade. Grill the chicken, covered, over medium heat for 5-6 minutes on each side or until juices run clear. Grill pineapple slices for 1 minute on each side. Spread mayonnaise mixture on rolls. Top with lettuce if desired, chicken and pineapple. **Yield:** 6 servings.

Sesame Chicken Kabobs

(Pictured above)

Cindy Novak, Antioch, California

This colorful dish is a favorite of mine for entertaining. I marinate the chicken and cut up the peppers the night before. Then the next day, I just have to assemble the kabobs and grill.

1/3 cup sherry *or* chicken broth
1/3 cup soy sauce
2 green onions, chopped
3 tablespoons apricot preserves
1 tablespoon vegetable oil
2 garlic cloves, minced
2 teaspoons minced fresh gingerroot
1/2 teaspoon hot pepper sauce
3 teaspoons sesame seeds, toasted, *divided*
1-1/2 pounds boneless skinless chicken breasts, cut into 1-inch cubes
1 medium sweet red pepper, cut into 1-inch pieces
1 medium sweet yellow pepper, cut into 1-inch pieces

In a bowl, combine the sherry or broth, soy sauce, onions, preserves, oil, garlic, ginger, hot pepper sauce and 1-1/2 teaspoons sesame seeds. Pour 1/3 cup into another bowl for basting; cover and refrigerate. Pour remaining marinade into a large resealable plastic bag; add chicken. Seal bag and turn to coat; refrigerate for 2-3 hours or overnight, turning occasionally.

Drain and discard marinade. On metal or soaked wooden skewers, alternately thread chicken and peppers. Grill, uncovered, over medium heat for 6 minutes, turning once. Baste with reserved marinade. Grill 5-10 minutes longer or until meat juices run clear, turning and basting frequently. Sprinkle with remaining sesame seeds. **Yield:** 6 servings.

Caribbean Chicken

(Pictured at right)

Rusty Collins, Orlando, Florida

You'd be hard-pressed to find a marinade that's this flavorful from any store! Add or subtract the jalapenos to suit your gang's taste, and you'll be grilling a new family favorite before you know it.

☑ Uses less fat, sugar or salt. Includes Nutritional Analysis and Diabetic Exchanges.

        1/2 cup lemon juice
        1/3 cup honey
          3 tablespoons canola oil
          6 green onions, sliced
          3 jalapeno peppers, seeded and chopped
          3 teaspoons dried thyme
        3/4 teaspoon salt
        1/4 teaspoon ground allspice
        1/4 teaspoon ground nutmeg
          6 boneless skinless chicken breast halves
            (1-1/2 pounds)

Place the first nine ingredients in a blender or food processor; cover and process until smooth. Pour 1/2 cup into a small bowl for basting; cover and refrigerate. Pour remaining marinade into a large resealable plastic bag; add chicken. Seal bag and turn to coat; refrigerate for up to 6 hours.

Drain and discard marinade. Coat grill rack with non-stick cooking spray before starting the grill. Grill chick-

en, covered, over medium heat for 4-6 minutes on each side or until juices run clear, basting frequently with the reserved marinade. **Yield:** 6 servings.

Nutritional Analysis: One serving (1 chicken breast half) equals 205 calories, 6 g fat (1 g saturated fat), 66 mg cholesterol, 272 mg sodium, 11 g carbohydrate, trace fiber, 27 g protein. **Diabetic Exchanges:** 3 lean meat, 1/2 starch.

Editor's Note: When cutting or seeding hot peppers, use rubber or plastic gloves to protect your hands. Avoid touching your face.

Southwestern Skewers

(Pictured at left)

Larry Smith, Youngstown, Ohio

Juicy chicken, cherry tomatoes, whole mushrooms and sweet peppers make these skewers filling. But it's the fresh garlic, chili powder, cumin and cayenne pepper that give them their zesty kick.

☑ Uses less fat, sugar or salt. Includes Nutritional Analysis and Diabetic Exchanges.

        1 bottle (8 ounces) reduced-fat Italian salad
          dressing

10 garlic cloves, minced
1 teaspoon white pepper
1 teaspoon chili powder
1 teaspoon ground cumin
1 teaspoon paprika
1/2 teaspoon cayenne pepper
1 medium green pepper, cut
  into 1-inch pieces
1 medium sweet red pepper, cut
  into 1-inch pieces
1 medium onion, cut into 1-inch pieces
8 large fresh mushrooms
8 cherry tomatoes
1 pound boneless skinless chicken breasts,
  cut into 1-inch cubes

In a bowl, combine the first seven ingredients; mix well. Pour half into a large resealable plastic bag; add the vegetables. Seal bag and turn to coat. Pour remaining marinade into another large resealable plastic bag; add the chicken. Seal bag and turn to coat. Refrigerate vegetables and chicken for at least 2-3 hours.

If grilling the kabobs, coat grill rack with nonstick cooking spray before starting the grill. Drain chicken, discarding the marinade. Drain the vegetables, reserving marinade for basting. On eight metal or soaked wooden skewers, alternately thread chicken and vegetables.

Grill, covered, over medium heat or broil 4-6 in. from the heat for 3-4 minutes on each side or until chicken is no longer pink and vegetables are tender, turning three times and basting frequently with reserved marinade. **Yield:** 4 servings.

Nutritional Analysis: One serving (2 kabobs) equals 231 calories, 7 g fat (1 g saturated fat), 63 mg cholesterol, 275 mg sodium, 15 g carbohydrate, 3 g fiber, 26 g protein. **Diabetic Exchanges:** 3 lean meat, 2 vegetable, 1 fat.

Common Herbs And Their Uses

- Basil: Licorice-like flavor is good in tomato, pasta, meat and vegetable dishes; also a traditional ingredient in pesto.
- Oregano: Peppery flavor is often used to season meats, soups, stews and chili.
- Parsley: Peps up salads, sauces and soups; also a popular garnish.
- Rosemary: Somewhat piney flavor is popular with roasted meats; also enhances tomato-based sauces.
- Tarragon: Mild licorice-like flavor seasons chicken recipes as well as salad dressings and creamy sauces.
- Thyme: Rich earthy taste complements stuffing, soups, stews, beef, chicken, fish and vegetables.

In a jar with tight-fitting lid, combine the first six ingredients; shake well. Pour half into a shallow glass dish (set remaining sauce aside). Dip chicken on both sides into sauce in dish; discard sauce.

Grill chicken, covered, over medium heat for 30 minutes, turning occasionally. Brush with reserved sauce. Continue basting and turning chicken several times for another 10-15 minutes or until juices run clear. **Yield:** 8 servings.

Grilled Lemon Chicken

(Pictured at right)

Linda Nilsen, Anoka, Minnesota

The secret behind the flavor that enhances this poultry dish is lemonade concentrate. This is a great recipe that I like to make for many summer gatherings.

1 can (6 ounces) frozen lemonade
  concentrate, thawed
1/3 cup soy sauce
1 garlic clove, minced
1 teaspoon seasoned salt
1/2 teaspoon celery salt
1/8 teaspoon garlic powder
2 broiler/fryer chickens (3 to 3-1/2 pounds
  each), quartered

and water in a small saucepan until smooth; stir in reserved marinade. Bring to a boil; cook and stir for 2 minutes or until thickened.

Remove and discard skin from chicken. Serve chicken over rice; drizzle with sauce. Garnish with green onions, orange slices and parsley if desired. **Yield:** 4 servings.

Nutritional Analysis: One serving (1 chicken breast half and 6 tablespoons sauce with 1 cup rice) equals 504 calories, 2 g fat (1 g saturated fat), 66 mg cholesterol, 755 mg sodium, 89 g carbohydrate, 1 g fiber, 32 g protein. **Diabetic Exchanges:** 4 lean meat, 3 starch, 1/2 fruit.

Honey Orange Chicken

(Pictured above)

Mary Hart Easterling, Santa Clarita, California

I couldn't get enough of the sweet-and-citrusy marinade that flavors this grilled chicken. So I saved some to drizzle on top. It's a refreshing addition to this chicken dish.

☑ Uses less fat, sugar or salt. Includes Nutritional Analysis and Diabetic Exchanges.

- 1 cup chicken broth
- 1 cup orange juice
- 1/2 cup honey
- 1 tablespoon lemon juice
- 1 tablespoon cider vinegar
- 1 tablespoon reduced-sodium soy sauce
- 1 teaspoon grated orange peel
- 1 teaspoon ground ginger
- 1/2 teaspoon salt
- 4 bone-in chicken breast halves (10 ounces each)
- 1 tablespoon cornstarch
- 2 tablespoons water
- 4 cups hot cooked rice
- Chopped green onions, orange slices and parsley sprigs, optional

In a saucepan, combine the first nine ingredients. Bring to a boil. Remove from the heat; cool. Pour 1-1/3 cups marinade into a large resealable plastic bag; add chicken. Seal bag and turn to coat; refrigerate for 4-8 hours or overnight, turning occasionally. Cover and refrigerate the remaining marinade.

Drain chicken, discarding marinade. Grill, covered, over medium heat for 12-15 minutes on each side or until juices run clear. Meanwhile, combine cornstarch

Grilled Italian Chicken

Joyce Pruitt, Jacksonville, Florida

This moist, tender chicken grills up in just minutes. With only two ingredients, the marinade couldn't be simpler, yet it gives the chicken wonderful flavor.

- 1 bottle (8 ounces) Italian salad dressing
- 3 tablespoons teriyaki sauce
- 8 boneless skinless chicken breast halves

In a bowl, combine salad dressing and teriyaki sauce. Remove 1/4 cup for basting; cover and refrigerate. Place chicken in a large resealable plastic bag; add remaining marinade. Seal bag and turn to coat; refrigerate for 8 hours or overnight, turning occasionally. Drain and discard marinade.

Grill chicken, covered, over medium heat for 3 minutes on each side. Baste with reserved marinade. Grill 3-4 minutes longer on each side or until juices run clear. **Yield:** 6 servings.

Barbecued Chicken

Joanne Shew Chuk, St. Benedict, Saskatchewan

If you're like me, you can never have enough delicious ways to grill chicken. The savory sauce in this recipe gives the chicken a wonderful herb flavor. It's easy to put together a great meal when you start with these juicy golden pieces.

☑ Uses less fat, sugar or salt. Includes Nutritional Analysis and Diabetic Exchanges.

- 1 broiler/fryer chicken (3-1/2 to 4 pounds), quartered
- 1/4 cup vinegar
- 1/4 cup margarine
- 1/4 cup water
- 1/4 teaspoon *each* dried thyme, oregano, rosemary and garlic powder

1/8 teaspoon salt
1/8 teaspoon pepper

Place chicken in a shallow glass dish. In a small saucepan, combine all remaining ingredients; bring to a gentle boil. Remove from the heat. Pour over chicken. Cover and refrigerate for 4 hours, turning once. Drain and discard marinade.

Grill the chicken, covered, over medium heat for 30-40 minutes or until the chicken juices run clear. **Yield:** 4 servings.

Nutritional Analysis: One serving (served without the skin) equals 224 calories, 225 mg sodium, 58 mg cholesterol, 1 g carbohydrate, 21 g protein, 14 g fat. **Diabetic Exchange:** 3 meat.

Yogurt-Marinated Chicken

(Pictured below)

Naheed Saleem, Stamford, Connecticut

This tender marinated chicken gets its zing from chili powder and cumin. For variety, I sometimes add a tablespoon of tomato paste to the marinade or replace the chili powder with chopped green chilies.

 Uses less fat, sugar or salt. Includes Nutritional Analysis and Diabetic Exchanges.

1/2 cup fat-free yogurt
3 garlic cloves, minced
2 tablespoons lemon juice
1 tablespoon canola oil
1 teaspoon sugar
1 teaspoon chili powder
1 tablespoon minced fresh gingerroot
1/2 teaspoon salt
1/2 teaspoon ground cumin
6 bone-in skinless chicken breast halves (6 ounces *each*)

In a large resealable plastic bag, combine the first nine ingredients; add the chicken. Seal bag and turn to coat; refrigerate for at least 8 hours or overnight.

Coat grill rack with nonstick cooking spray before starting the grill for indirect heat. Drain and discard marinade.

Grill the chicken, covered, bone side down over indirect medium heat for 20 minutes. Turn; grill 20-30 minutes longer or until the chicken juices run clear. **Yield:** 6 servings.

Nutritional Analysis: One serving (1 chicken breast half) equals 149 calories, 4 g fat (1 g saturated fat), 68 mg cholesterol, 163 mg sodium, 2 g carbohydrate, trace fiber, 25 g protein. **Diabetic Exchange:** 3 lean meat.

Plum-Glazed Chicken Kabobs

(Pictured below)

Nancy Morrison, Midlothian, Virginia

These creative kabobs make a great first impression. I brought them to a neighborhood dinner when we moved to our new home. People couldn't wait 'til dinner and started snatching them as soon as I walked in the door. They just couldn't resist the tantalizing aroma.

✓ Uses less fat, sugar or salt. Includes Nutritional Analysis and Diabetic Exchanges.

    1 cup plum jam
    3 tablespoons reduced-sodium soy sauce
    1 tablespoon sherry *or* chicken broth
  1/4 teaspoon garlic powder
  1/4 teaspoon ground ginger
    1 pound boneless skinless chicken breasts, cubed
    1 can (20 ounces) pineapple chunks, drained
    1 large green pepper, cut into 1-inch pieces
    1 teaspoon cornstarch
    3 cups cooked rice

In a saucepan, combine the first five ingredients; heat on low until jam is melted. In a large resealable plastic bag, combine the chicken, pineapple and green pepper; add plum mixture. Seal bag and turn to coat; refrigerate for at least 2 hours.

Place cornstarch in a small saucepan; drain marinade into saucepan. Stir until smooth. Bring to a rolling boil over medium heat; cook and stir for 1 minute or until thickened. Remove from the heat; set aside.

On 12 metal or soaked wooden skewers, alternately thread chicken, pineapple and green pepper. Grill over medium heat or place skewers on a broiler pan 3-4 in. from the heat. Grill or broil for 3 minutes, turning once. Baste with plum glaze. Grill or broil 4-6 minutes longer or until chicken juices run clear, turning and basting frequently. Serve over rice with any remaining glaze. **Yield:** 4 servings.

Nutritional Analysis: One serving (3 skewers with 3/4 cup rice) equals 615 calories, 2 g fat (trace saturated fat), 66 mg cholesterol, 570 mg sodium, 108 g carbohydrate, 2 g fiber, 31 g protein.

Zesty Mustard Chicken

(Pictured above)

Michael Everidge, Morristown, Tennessee

Whether you're grilling a broiler chicken or chicken breasts, consider this lip-smacking glaze. There are only four ingredients in the honey-mustard sauce, so you can whip it up in minutes.

✓ Uses less fat, sugar or salt. Includes Nutritional Analysis and Diabetic Exchanges.

  1/2 cup prepared mustard
  1/2 cup honey
    1 tablespoon salt-free seasoning blend
    1 tablespoon Worcestershire sauce
    1 broiler/fryer chicken (3 pounds), cut in half

In a bowl, combine the first four ingredients; mix well. Carefully loosen the skin of the chicken; spoon some of the mustard sauce under the skin.

Coat grill rack with nonstick cooking spray before starting the grill. Place chicken skin side up on grill rack. Grill, covered, over indirect medium heat for 20 minutes. Turn; grill 20-30 minutes longer or until juices run clear, basting occasionally with remaining mustard sauce. Remove chicken skin; cut into serving-size pieces. **Yield:** 6 servings.

Nutritional Analysis: One serving equals 261 calories, 7 g fat (2 g saturated fat), 72 mg cholesterol, 334 mg sodium, 25 g carbohydrate, 1 g fiber, 25 g protein. **Diabetic Exchanges:** 3 lean meat, 1-1/2 starch.

Peanut Butter Chicken Skewers

(Pictured below)

Jeanne Bennett, North Richland Hills, Texas

Most people associate peanut butter only with snacks or desserts. This fantastic dish proves it also makes a mouth-watering sauce for chicken.

- 1/2 cup creamy peanut butter
- 1/2 cup water
- 1/4 cup soy sauce
- 4 garlic cloves, minced
- 3 tablespoons lemon juice
- 2 tablespoons brown sugar
- 3/4 teaspoon ground ginger
- 1/2 teaspoon crushed red pepper flakes
- 4 boneless skinless chicken breast halves
- 2 cups shredded red cabbage

Sliced green onion tops

In a saucepan, combine the first eight ingredients; cook and stir over medium-high heat for 5 minutes or until smooth. Reserve half of the sauce. Slice the chicken lengthwise into 1-in. strips; thread onto the skewers (if using bamboo skewers, soak them in water for at least 20 minutes).

Grill, uncovered, over medium-hot heat for 2 minutes; turn and brush with peanut butter sauce. Continue turning and basting for 4-6 minutes or until juices run clear.

Place cabbage on a serving plate; top with chicken. Sprinkle with onion tops. Serve with reserved sauce. **Yield:** 4 servings.

Maple-Glazed Chicken Wings

Janice Henck, Clarkston, Georgia

Some wonderful maple syrup I brought back from my last trip to Vermont is what inspired the recipe. These wings have been a hit with family and friends.

- 2 to 3 pounds whole chicken wings
- 1 cup maple syrup
- 2/3 cup chili sauce
- 1/2 cup finely chopped onion
- 2 tablespoons Dijon mustard
- 2 teaspoons Worcestershire sauce
- 1/4 to 1/2 teaspoon crushed red pepper flakes

Cut chicken wings into three sections; discard wing tip section. In a large resealable plastic bag or shallow glass container, combine remaining ingredients. Reserve 1 cup for basting and refrigerate.

Add chicken to remaining marinade and turn to coat. Seal bag or cover container; refrigerate for 4 hours, turning occasionally. Drain and discard marinade.

Grill chicken, covered, over medium heat for 12-16 minutes, turning occasionally. Brush with reserved marinade. Grill, uncovered, for 8-10 minutes or until juices run clear, basting and turning several times. **Yield:** 6-8 servings.

Orange Chicken And Veggies

(Pictured below)

Violet Klause, Onoway, Alberta

A mild maple marinade seasons this summery supper. It has a great combination featuring chicken, peppers, zucchini, pineapple and oranges.

✓ Uses less fat, sugar or salt. Includes Nutritional Analysis and Diabetic Exchanges.

- 1 can (6 ounces) frozen orange juice concentrate, thawed
- 3/4 cup maple syrup
- 4 teaspoons canola oil
- 3/4 teaspoon curry powder
- 1/4 teaspoon cayenne pepper
- 6 boneless skinless chicken breast halves (1-1/2 pounds)
- 2 medium sweet red peppers, halved and seeded
- 1 medium green pepper, halved and seeded
- 3 medium zucchini, halved lengthwise
- 1 fresh pineapple, peeled and cut into 1/2-inch slices
- 2 unpeeled medium oranges, cut into 1/2-inch slices

In a bowl, combine the orange juice concentrate, syrup, oil, curry and cayenne. Place chicken in a large resealable plastic bag; add half of the marinade. Seal bag and turn to coat.

Place the peppers, zucchini, pineapple and oranges in another resealable bag; add remaining marinade. Seal bag and turn to coat. Refrigerate chicken and vegetables for 8 hours or overnight, turning occasionally.

Drain chicken, discarding marinade. Drain vegetables and fruits, reserving marinade for basting. Grill the chicken, vegetables and fruits, uncovered, over medium heat for 3 minutes on each side. Baste with reserved marinade. Continue turning and basting 6-8 minutes longer or until chicken juices run clear, vegetables are tender and fruits are golden brown. **Yield:** 6 servings.

Nutritional Analysis: One serving (1 chicken breast with 3/4 cup vegetable mixture) equals 320 calories, 5 g fat (1 g saturated fat), 73 mg cholesterol, 71 mg sodium, 40 g carbohydrate, 4 g fiber, 29 g protein. **Diabetic Exchanges:** 3-1/2 very lean meat, 2 vegetable, 2 fruit, 1/2 fat.

Grilled Chicken Cordon Bleu

(Pictured at right)

Shawna McCutcheon
Homer City, Pennsylvania

These special chicken bundles are absolutely de-licious. You can assemble them in advance and keep them in the fridge. Then just place them on the grill.

- 6 boneless skinless chicken breast halves
- 6 slices Swiss cheese
- 6 thin slices deli ham
- 3 tablespoons olive oil
- 3/4 cup seasoned bread crumbs

Flatten the chicken to 1/4-in. thickness. Place a slice of cheese and ham on each to within 1/4 in. of edges. Fold in half; secure with thin metal skewers or toothpicks. Brush with oil and roll in bread crumbs. Grill, covered, over medium-hot heat for 15-18 minutes or until juices run clear. **Yield:** 6 servings.

Citrus Chicken Kabobs

Suzi Sisson, San Diego, California

I've been experimenting with lighter evening meals. My family loves how fresh these appealing glazed kabobs taste.

✓ Uses less fat, sugar or salt. Includes Nutritional Analysis and Diabetic Exchanges.

- 1 pound fresh broccoli, broken into florets
- 2 large navel oranges
- 1 pound boneless skinless chicken breasts, cut into 1-inch cubes
- 4 plum tomatoes, quartered
- 1 large onion, cut into wedges

GLAZE:
- 1/4 cup barbecue sauce
- 2 tablespoons lemon juice
- 2 tablespoons reduced-sodium soy sauce
- 2 tablespoons honey

Place 1 in. of water in a large saucepan; add broccoli. Bring to a boil. Reduce heat; cover and simmer for 3-4 minutes or until crisp-tender. Drain. Cut each orange in-to eight wedges. On eight metal or soaked wooden skewers, alternately thread chicken, vegetables and or-anges. In a small bowl, combine glaze ingredients.

If grilling the kabobs, coat grill rack with nonstick cooking spray before starting the grill. Grill kabobs, uncovered, over medium heat or broil 4-6 in. from the heat for 5-7 minutes on each side or until chicken juices run clear, turning once. Brush frequently with glaze. **Yield:** 4 servings.

Nutritional Analysis: One serving (2 kabobs) equals 278 calories, 3 g fat (1 g saturated fat), 63 mg choles-terol, 568 mg sodium, 38 g carbohydrate, 8 g fiber, 28 g protein. **Diabetic Exchanges:** 3 very lean meat, 3 vegetable, 1-1/2 fruit.

Merry Marinades

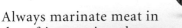

Always marinate meat in the refrigerator in a glass con-tainer or resealable plastic bag. Generally, you should never reuse marinades. If marinating meat, set aside a portion before adding uncooked foods.

Honey-Lime Grilled Chicken

Dorothy Smith, El Dorado, Arkansas

You won't have to pack a lot of supplies to stir up this easy marinade. It requires only three ingredients!

- 1/2 cup honey
- 1/3 cup soy sauce
- 1/4 cup lime juice
- 4 boneless skinless chicken breast halves

In a resealable plastic bag or shallow glass container, combine the honey, soy sauce and lime juice; mix well. Add chicken and turn to coat. Seal or cover and refrigerate for 30-45 minutes. Drain and discard mari-nade. Grill chicken, uncovered, over medium heat for 6-7 minutes on each side or until juices run clear. **Yield:** 4 servings.

Brown Rice Salad with Grilled Chicken

(Pictured below)

Glenda Harper, Cable, Ohio

This delightful dish is nutritious, simple to fix and brightens up any buffet table. It's a terrific way to use up leftover chicken, and you can add veggies according to your family's liking.

 Uses less fat, sugar or salt. Includes Nutritional Analysis and Diabetic Exchanges.

    3 cups cooked brown rice
    2 cups cubed grilled chicken breast
    2 medium tart apples, diced
    1 medium sweet red pepper, diced
    2 celery ribs, finely chopped
  2/3 cup chopped green onions
  1/2 cup chopped pecans
    3 tablespoons minced fresh parsley
  1/4 cup cider vinegar
    3 tablespoons canola oil
    1 tablespoon lemon juice
    1 teaspoon salt
  1/4 teaspoon pepper
Lettuce leaves, optional

In a large bowl, combine the rice, chicken, apples, red pepper, celery, onions, pecans and parsley.

In a jar with a tight-fitting lid, combine the vinegar, oil, lemon juice, salt and pepper, and shake well.

Pour over the rice mixture and toss to coat. Serve immediately or refrigerate. Serve in a lettuce-lined bowl if desired. **Yield:** 9 servings.

Montego Bay Chicken

(Pictured above)

Julie DeMatteo, Clementon, New Jersey

You don't need high-fat ingredients to make grilled chicken taste good. The marinade flavors and tenderizes the meat.

✓ Uses less fat, sugar or salt. Includes Nutritional Analysis and Diabetic Exchanges.

  1/4 cup reduced-sodium soy sauce
  1/4 cup orange juice
    2 tablespoons brown sugar
    2 garlic cloves, minced
    1 teaspoon hot pepper sauce
    1 teaspoon rum extract
    1 teaspoon minced fresh gingerroot
    4 boneless skinless chicken breast halves
       (4 ounces *each*)

In a large resealable plastic bag, combine the soy sauce, orange juice, brown sugar, minced garlic, hot pepper sauce, rum extract and minced gingerroot. Add the chicken. Seal bag and turn to coat; refrigerate for at least 2 hours.

Drain and discard marinade. Coat grill rack with nonstick cooking spray before starting the grill. Grill chicken, uncovered, over indirect medium heat for 6-8 minutes on each side or until juices run clear. **Yield:** 4 servings.

Nutritional Analysis: One serving equals 138 calories, 1 g fat (trace saturated fat), 66 mg cholesterol, 379 mg sodium, 3 g carbohydrate, trace fiber, 27 g protein. **Diabetic Exchange:** 3 lean meat.

Nutritional Analysis: One serving (1 cup) equals 236 calories, 11 g fat (1 g saturated fat), 26 mg cholesterol, 295 mg sodium, 23 g carbohydrate, 3 g fiber, 12 g protein. **Diabetic Exchanges:** 1-1/2 fat, 1 starch, 1 lean meat, 1/2 fruit.

Campfire Chicken Stew

Florence Kreis, Beach Park, Illinois

My family loves these chicken stew packets on camping trips, but they're equally good on our backyard grill.

- 1 broiler/fryer chicken (3-1/2 to 4 pounds), cut up
- 3 to 4 medium potatoes, peeled and sliced
- 1 cup thinly sliced carrots
- 1 medium green pepper, sliced
- 1 can (10-3/4 ounces) condensed cream of mushroom soup, undiluted
- 1/4 cup water
- 1/2 teaspoon salt
- 1/4 teaspoon pepper

Grill chicken, uncovered, over medium heat for 3 minutes on each side. Place two pieces of chicken each on only four pieces of heavy-duty foil (about 18 in. x 12 in.).

Divide the potatoes, carrots and green pepper between the four pieces of foil. Top each with 2 tablespoons soup, 1 tablespoon water, salt and pepper. Fold the foil around mixture and seal tightly.

Grill, covered, over medium heat for 20 minutes; turn and grill 20-25 minutes longer or until vegetables are tender and chicken juices run clear. **Yield:** 4 servings.

Apple Thyme Chicken

(Pictured above right)

Peter Halferty, Corpus Christi, Texas

Apples and chicken may seem like an unusual combination, but they make a wonderful meal. The thyme marinade gives a boost of flavor.

✓ Uses less fat, sugar or salt. Includes Nutritional Analysis and Diabetic Exchanges.

- 6 tablespoons apple juice
- 6 tablespoons lemon juice
- 4-1/2 teaspoons cider vinegar
- 4-1/2 teaspoons canola oil
- 1-1/2 teaspoons dried thyme
- 4 boneless skinless chicken breast halves (4 ounces *each*)

- 2 medium Golden Delicious *or* other all-purpose apples, peeled and quartered
- 1 tablespoon honey

SAUCE:
- 2 teaspoons cornstarch
- 1/4 teaspoon dried thyme
- 3/4 cup apple juice

In a bowl, combine the first five ingredients; mix well. Pour half of the marinade into a large resealable plastic bag; add chicken. Seal bag and turn to coat; refrigerate for at least 2 hours. Cover and refrigerate remaining marinade.

Coat the grill rack with nonstick cooking spray before starting the grill. Drain and discard the marinade from chicken. Dip the apples in the reserved marinade and set aside. Combine the honey with the remaining marinade.

Grill chicken, covered, over medium heat for 4-6 minutes on each side or until juices run clear, basting frequently with the honey marinade. Grill apples, uncovered, for 3-5 minutes, basting and turning frequently or until lightly browned.

In a saucepan, combine the cornstarch, thyme and apple juice until blended. Bring to a boil; cook and stir for 2 minutes or until thickened. Slice the grilled apples; stir into sauce. Serve with chicken. **Yield:** 4 servings.

Nutritional Analysis: One serving (1 chicken breast half with 1/4 cup sauce) equals 226 calories, 3 g fat (1 g saturated fat), 66 mg cholesterol, 76 mg sodium, 22 g carbohydrate, 1 g fiber, 26 g protein. **Diabetic Exchanges:** 3 lean meat, 1-1/2 fruit.

4 Slow-Cooked Favorites

Mexican Chicken Soup

(Pictured at left)

Marlene Kane, Lainesburg, Michigan

This zesty dish is loaded with chicken, corn and black beans. As a busy mom of three children, I'm always looking for dinner recipes that can be prepared in the morning.

✓ Uses less fat, sugar or salt. Includes Nutritional Analysis and Diabetic Exchanges.

- 1-1/2 pounds boneless skinless chicken breasts, cubed
- 2 teaspoons canola oil
- 1/2 cup water
- 1 envelope reduced-sodium taco seasoning
- 1 can (32 ounces) V8 juice
- 1 jar (16 ounces) salsa
- 1 can (15 ounces) black beans, rinsed and drained
- 1 package (10 ounces) frozen corn, thawed
- 6 tablespoons reduced-fat cheddar cheese
- 6 tablespoons reduced-fat sour cream
- 2 tablespoons chopped fresh cilantro

In a large nonstick skillet, saute chicken in oil until no longer pink. Add water and taco seasoning; simmer until chicken is well coated. Transfer to a slow cooker.

Add V8 juice, salsa, beans and corn; mix well. Cover and cook on low for 3-4 hours or until heated through. Serve with cheese, sour cream and cilantro. **Yield:** 6 servings.

Nutritional Analysis: One serving (1-1/2 cups with 1 tablespoon each cheese and sour cream and 1 teaspoon cilantro) equals 345 calories, 6 g fat (2 g saturated fat), 75 mg cholesterol, 1,385 mg sodium, 35 g carbohydrate, 7 g fiber, 36 g protein. **Diabetic Exchanges:** 4 very lean meat, 2 vegetable, 1-1/2 starch, 1/2 fat.

Stuffed Chicken Rolls

Jean Sherwood, Kenneth City, Florida

The wonderful aroma of this moist, delicious chicken cooking triggers our appetites every time! The ham and cheese rolled inside is a tasty surprise. When I prepared this im-pressive main dish for a church luncheon, I received many compliments. The rolls are nice served over hot cooked rice or pasta.

- 6 large boneless skinless chicken breast halves
- 6 slices fully cooked ham
- 6 slices Swiss cheese
- 1/4 cup all-purpose flour
- 1/4 cup grated Parmesan cheese
- 1/2 teaspoon rubbed sage
- 1/4 teaspoon paprika
- 1/4 teaspoon pepper
- 1/4 cup vegetable oil
- 1 can (10-3/4 ounces) condensed cream of chicken soup, undiluted
- 1/2 cup chicken broth
- Chopped fresh parsley, optional

Flatten chicken to 1/8-in. thickness. Place ham and cheese on each breast. Roll up and tuck in ends; secure with a toothpick. Combine the flour, Parmesan cheese, sage, paprika and pepper; coat chicken on all sides. Cover and refrigerate for 1 hour.

In a large skillet, brown chicken in oil over medium-high heat. Transfer to a 5-qt. slow cooker. Combine soup and broth; pour over chicken. Cover and cook on low for 4-5 hours. Remove toothpicks. Garnish with parsley if desired. **Yield:** 6 servings.

Saucy Apricot Chicken

Dee Gray, Kokomo, Indiana

Four ingredients are all you'll need for this tender chicken entree. The tangy glaze is just as wonderful with ham or turkey, plus it's so very easy to make with a few handy ingredients. Leftovers reheat nicely in the microwave.

- 6 boneless skinless chicken breast halves (about 1-1/2 pounds)
- 2 jars (12 ounces *each*) apricot preserves
- 1 envelope onion soup mix
- Hot cooked rice

Place chicken in a slow cooker. Combine the preserves and soup mix; spoon over chicken. Cover and cook on low for 4-5 hours or until tender. Serve over rice. **Yield:** 6 servings.

Rosemary Cashew Chicken

(Pictured above)

Ruth Andrewson, Peck, Idaho

With its fresh herb flavor and crunchy cashews, this elegant entree is mouth-watering.

 1 broiler/fryer chicken (3 to 4 pounds), cut up and skin removed
 1 medium onion, thinly sliced
 1/3 cup orange juice concentrate
 1 teaspoon dried rosemary, crushed
 1 teaspoon salt
 1/4 teaspoon cayenne pepper
 2 tablespoons all-purpose flour
 3 tablespoons water
 1/4 to 1/2 cup chopped cashews
Hot cooked pasta

Place chicken in a slow cooker. Combine the onion, orange juice concentrate, rosemary, salt and cayenne; pour over chicken. Cover and cook on low for 4-5 hours or until chicken juices run clear.

Remove chicken and keep warm. In a saucepan, combine flour and water until smooth. Stir in cooking juices. Bring to a boil; cook and stir for 2 minutes or until thickened. Stir in cashews. Pour over chicken. Serve with pasta. **Yield:** 4-6 servings.

Slow-Cooked Orange Chicken

Nancy Wit, Fremont, Nebraska

I created this recipe in an effort to prepare a dish lower in calories and fat. A hint of orange gives the chicken a deli-cious flavor. This is a favorite of mine.

 Uses less fat, sugar or salt. Includes Nutritional Analysis and Diabetic Exchanges.

 1 broiler/fryer chicken (3 pounds), cut up and skin removed
 3 cups orange juice
 1 cup chopped celery
 1 cup chopped green pepper
 1 can (4 ounces) mushroom stems and pieces, drained
 4 teaspoons dried minced onion
 1 tablespoon minced fresh parsley *or* 1 teaspoon dried parsley flakes
 1/2 teaspoon salt, optional
 1/4 teaspoon pepper
 3 tablespoons cornstarch
 3 tablespoons cold water
Hot cooked rice, optional

Combine the first nine ingredients in a slow cooker. Cover and cook on low for 4 hours or until meat juices run clear. Combine cornstarch and water until smooth;

stir into cooking juices. Cover and cook on high for 30-45 minutes or until thickened. Serve over rice if desired. **Yield:** 4 servings.

Nutritional Analysis: One serving (prepared without salt; calculated without rice) equals 306 calories, 189 mg sodium, 70 mg cholesterol, 31 g carbohydrate, 23 g protein, 10 g fat. **Diabetic Exchanges:** 3 lean meat, 1 fruit, 1 starch.

Fruited Chicken

(Pictured below)

Mirien Church, Aurora, Colorado

With three young children, I appreciate the ease of preparing entrees like this with my slow cooker. The combination of fruity flavors in this chicken dish is unique and tasty. My husband loves having home-cooked meals each night, and this one is always a hit!

- 1 **large onion, sliced**
- 6 **boneless skinless chicken breast halves**
- 1/3 **cup orange juice**
- 2 **tablespoons soy sauce**
- 2 **tablespoons Worcestershire sauce**
- 2 **tablespoons Dijon mustard**
- 1 **tablespoon grated orange peel**
- 2 **garlic cloves, minced**
- 1/2 **cup chopped dried apricots**
- 1/2 **cup dried cranberries**

Hot cooked rice

Place onion and chicken in a 5-qt. slow cooker. Combine the orange juice, soy sauce, Worcestershire sauce, mustard, orange peel and garlic; pour over the chicken.

Sprinkle with apricots and cranberries. Cover and cook on low for 7-8 hours or until chicken juices run clear. Serve over rice. **Yield:** 6 servings.

Lemon Chicken

(Pictured above)

Walter Powell, Wilmington, Delaware

Garlic, oregano and lemon juice give spark to this memorable main dish. It's easy to fix—just brown the chicken in a skillet, then let the slow cooker do the work.

- 6 **bone-in chicken breast halves (about 3 pounds), skin removed**
- 1 **teaspoon dried oregano**
- 1/2 **teaspoon seasoned salt**
- 1/4 **teaspoon pepper**
- 2 **tablespoons butter**
- 1/4 **cup water**
- 3 **tablespoons lemon juice**
- 2 **garlic cloves, minced**
- 1 **teaspoon chicken bouillon granules**
- 2 **teaspoons minced fresh parsley**

Hot cooked rice

Pat chicken dry with paper towels. Combine the oregano, seasoned salt and pepper; rub over chicken. In a skillet over medium heat, brown the chicken in butter; transfer to a 5-qt. slow cooker. Add water, lemon juice, garlic and bouillon to the skillet; bring to a boil, stirring to loosen browned bits. Pour over chicken.

Cover and cook on low for 3-4 hours. Baste chicken. Add parsley. Cover and cook 15-30 minutes longer or until meat juices run clear. If desired, thicken cooking juices and serve over chicken and rice. **Yield:** 6 servings.

Creamy Chicken Fettuccine

(Pictured below)

Melissa Cowser, Greenville, Texas

Canned soup and process cheese hurry along the assembly of this creamy sauce loaded with delicious chunks of chicken.

- 1-1/2 pounds boneless skinless chicken breasts, cut into cubes
- 1/2 teaspoon garlic powder
- 1/2 teaspoon onion powder
- 1/8 teaspoon pepper
- 1 can (10-3/4 ounces) condensed cream of chicken soup, undiluted
- 1 can (10-3/4 ounces) condensed cream of celery soup, undiluted
- 4 ounces process cheese (Velveeta), cubed
- 1 can (2-1/4 ounces) sliced ripe olives, drained
- 1 jar (2 ounces) diced pimientos, drained, optional
- 1 package (16 ounces) spinach fettuccine *or* spaghetti

Thin breadsticks, optional

Place the chicken in a slow cooker; sprinkle with garlic powder, onion powder and pepper. Top with soups. Cover and cook on high for 3-4 hours or until chicken juices run clear.

Stir in cheese, olives and pimientos if desired. Cover and cook until cheese is melted. Meanwhile, cook fettuccine according to package directions; drain. Serve with the chicken and breadsticks if desired. **Yield:** 6 servings.

Chicken Dinner

Jenet Cattar, Neptune Beach, Florida

I love using my slow cooker because it's so convenient. This meal-in-one, which includes juicy chicken and tasty veggies in a creamy sauce, is ready to eat when I get home from the office.

- 6 medium red potatoes, cut into chunks
- 4 medium carrots, cut into 1/2-inch pieces
- 4 boneless skinless chicken breast halves
- 1 can (10-3/4 ounces) condensed cream of chicken soup, undiluted
- 1 can (10-3/4 ounces) condensed cream of mushroom soup, undiluted
- 1/8 teaspoon garlic salt
- 2 to 4 tablespoons mashed potato flakes, optional

Place the potatoes and carrots in a slow cooker. Top with the chicken. Combine the soups and garlic salt; pour over chicken. Cover and cook on low for 8 hours. To thicken if desired, stir potato flakes into the gravy and cook 30 minutes longer. **Yield:** 4 servings.

Nostalgic Chicken And Dumplings

(Pictured at right)

Brenda Edwards, Hereford, Arizona

Enjoy old-fashioned goodness featuring tender chicken, wonderfully light dumplings and a full-flavored sauce.

✓ Uses less fat, sugar or salt. Includes Nutritional Analysis and Diabetic Exchanges.

    6 bone-in chicken breast halves (10 ounces
      each), skin removed
    2 whole cloves
   12 frozen pearl or small whole onions, thawed
    1 bay leaf
    1 garlic clove, minced
  1/2 teaspoon each salt, dried thyme and dried
      marjoram
  1/4 teaspoon pepper
  1/2 cup reduced-sodium chicken broth
  1/2 cup white wine or additional chicken broth
    3 tablespoons cornstarch
  1/4 cup cold water
  1/2 teaspoon browning sauce, optional
    1 cup reduced-fat biscuit/baking mix
    6 tablespoons fat-free milk
    1 tablespoon minced fresh parsley

Place the chicken in a slow cooker. Insert cloves into an onion; add to slow cooker. Add bay leaf and remaining onions. Sprinkle chicken with garlic, salt, thyme, marjoram and pepper. Pour broth and wine or additional broth over chicken mixture. Cover and cook on low for 4-1/2 to 5 hours or until chicken juices run clear and a meat thermometer reads 170°.

Remove chicken and keep warm. Discard cloves and bay leaf. Increase temperature to high. In a small bowl, combine cornstarch, water and browning sauce if desired until smooth. Stir into slow cooker.

In another bowl, combine the biscuit mix, milk and parsley. Drop by tablespoonfuls onto simmering liquid. Cover and simmer for 20-25 minutes or until a toothpick inserted into dumplings comes out clean (do not lift cover while simmering). Serve dumplings and gravy over chicken. **Yield:** 6 servings.

Nutritional Analysis: One serving equals 295 calories, 5 g fat (1 g saturated fat), 89 mg cholesterol, 561 mg sodium, 24 g carbohydrate, 2 g fiber, 36 g protein. **Diabetic Exchanges:** 4 lean meat, 1 starch, 1 vegetable.

Slow Cooker Tip

Be sure the lid on your slow cooker is seated properly. It is the steam from cooking that creates a seal.

Tangy Tender Chicken

Milton Schutz, Pandora, Ohio

Brown sugar, garlic and ginger provide the traditional sweet-sour flavor in this chicken medley. The aroma is heavenly after working outside all day, and it's delicious and satisfying served over rice.

    1 pound baby carrots
    1 medium green pepper, cut into 1/2-inch
      strips
    1 medium onion, cut into wedges
    6 boneless skinless chicken breast halves
    1 can (20 ounces) pineapple chunks
  1/3 cup packed brown sugar
    1 tablespoon soy sauce
    2 teaspoons chicken bouillon granules
  1/2 teaspoon salt
  1/2 teaspoon ground ginger
  1/4 teaspoon garlic powder
    3 tablespoons cornstarch
  1/4 cup cold water
Hot cooked rice

In a slow cooker, layer carrots, green pepper and onion. Top with the chicken. Drain pineapple, reserving juice. Place pineapple over chicken. Add brown sugar, soy sauce, bouillon, salt, ginger and garlic powder to pineapple juice; pour over pineapple. Cover and cook on low for 8-9 hours.

Combine cornstarch and water until smooth; gradually stir into cooking juices. Cook 30 minutes longer or until sauce is thickened, stirring once. Serve over rice. **Yield:** 4-6 servings.

5 Cooking for Two

Baked Pineapple Chicken

(Pictured at left)

Marcille Meyer, Battle Creek, Nebraska

Ginger and crushed pineapple flavor tender juicy chicken in this main dish. Orange marmalade and lemon juice add just a hint of refreshing citrus tang.

✓ Uses less fat, sugar or salt. Includes Nutritional Analysis and Diabetic Exchanges.

- 1/4 **cup chicken broth**
- 3 **tablespoons reduced-sodium soy sauce**
- 1 **teaspoon ground ginger,** *divided*
- 2 **bone-in chicken breast halves (6 ounces** *each*), **skin removed**
- 1 **can (8 ounces) unsweetened crushed pineapple, undrained**
- 1 **teaspoon cornstarch**
- 2 **teaspoons orange marmalade**
- 1 **teaspoon lemon juice**

In a large resealable plastic bag, combine the broth, soy sauce and 1/2 teaspoon ginger; add chicken. Seal bag and turn to coat; refrigerate for 2 hours, turning occasionally.

Drain pineapple, reserving 1/2 cup juice; set aside 1/4 cup pineapple (refrigerate remaining pineapple and juice for another use). In a saucepan, combine cornstarch and reserved pineapple juice until smooth.

Stir in the pineapple, orange marmalade, lemon juice and remaining ginger. Bring the mixture to a boil; cook and stir for 1-2 minutes or until thickened.

Drain and discard marinade. Place chicken in a 9-in. square baking dish coated with nonstick cooking spray. Top with pineapple mixture. Bake, uncovered, at 350° for 45-50 minutes or until chicken juices run clear. **Yield:** 2 servings.

Downsized Chicken

If you often cook for one or two, you can prepare a larger amount of the chicken called for in a recipe to use in future recipes. Or, freeze small amounts of leftover chicken until you have enough for a potpie, casserole or another satisfying meal.

Nutritional Analysis: One serving equals 207 calories, 3 g fat (1 g saturated fat), 68 mg cholesterol, 330 mg sodium, 18 g carbohydrate, 1 g fiber, 26 g protein. **Diabetic Exchanges:** 3 lean meat, 1 fruit.

Mushroom Cream Chicken

Marian Slattery, Whitewater, Wisconsin

This special dish stars wonderfully tender chicken smothered in a delicious mushroom cream sauce. It tastes like you fussed for hours to make it, but it's really simple to prepare.

✓ Uses less fat, sugar or salt. Includes Nutritional Analysis and Diabetic Exchanges.

- 2 **boneless skinless chicken breast halves (1/2 pound)**
- 3 **tablespoons all-purpose flour,** *divided*
- 2 **teaspoons butter**
- 1 **teaspoon canola oil**
- 1 **cup sliced fresh mushrooms**
- 1 **tablespoon sliced green onion**
- 1 **garlic clove, minced**
- 3/4 **cup chicken broth**
- 1/2 **cup Madeira wine** *or* **additional chicken broth**
- 1 **tablespoon fat-free half-and-half cream**

Flatten chicken to 1/4-in. thickness. Dredge in 2 tablespoons flour. In a nonstick skillet, brown chicken in butter and oil over medium heat for 2-3 minutes on each side or until juices run clear. Remove chicken and set aside.

In the same skillet, saute the mushrooms, green onion and garlic for 2 minutes or until tender. Sprinkle with remaining flour and stir to blend. Gradually add broth and wine or additional broth. Bring to a boil; cook and stir for 2 minutes or until thickened. Reduce heat; add the cream. Return chicken to skillet. Cook for 2-3 minutes or until chicken is heated through (do not boil). **Yield:** 2 servings.

Nutritional Analysis: One serving (1 chicken breast half with 3/4 cup sauce) equals 327 calories, 9 g fat (3 g saturated fat), 78 mg cholesterol, 457 mg sodium, 18 g carbohydrate, 1 g fiber, 29 g protein. **Diabetic Exchanges:** 3 lean meat, 1 starch, 1 vegetable, 1 fat.

sodium, 12 g carbohydrate, 3 g fiber, 28 g protein. **Diabetic Exchanges:** 3 lean meat, 2 vegetable, 1/2 fat.

Spanish Chicken and Rice

(Pictured below)

Mary Nelms, Jacksonville, Florida

I've had this recipe for more than 50 years and have probably made it hundreds of times. I like this dish because it can be prepared quickly. The portions are just right for two people, and any leftovers are just as delicious the next day.

    2 **tablespoons all-purpose flour**
    1 **teaspoon salt,** *divided*
 1/4 **teaspoon pepper**
    2 **bone-in chicken breast halves**
    1 **tablespoon butter**
 1/2 **cup chopped onion**
 1/4 **cup chopped green pepper**
    1 **garlic clove, minced**
    1 **jar (2-1/2 ounces) sliced pimientos, drained**
 1/2 **cup uncooked rice**
1-1/4 **cups chicken broth**
 1/2 **teaspoon ground turmeric**
 1/8 **to 1/4 teaspoon chili powder**

Combine flour, 1/2 teaspoon of salt and pepper in a large resealable plastic bag. Add chicken and shake

Gingered Chicken Stir-Fry

(Pictured above)

Donna Sauvageau, Detroit Lakes, Minnesota

Ginger and soy sauce give eye-opening flavor to this colorful stir-fry. Plus you get a nice blend of vegetables in this tasty meal.

✓ Uses less fat, sugar or salt. Includes Nutritional Analysis and Diabetic Exchanges.

   1 **tablespoon ketchup**
   1 **tablespoon minced fresh gingerroot**
   2 **tablespoons reduced-sodium soy sauce**
   2 **garlic cloves, minced**
 3/4 **pound boneless skinless chicken breasts, cut into thin strips**
   1 **large green pepper, sliced**
   1 **large sweet red pepper, sliced**
   6 **green onions, sliced**
   2 **teaspoons canola oil,** *divided*
   2 **teaspoons sesame** *or* **additional canola oil,** *divided*
Hot cooked rice, optional

In a large resealable plastic bag, combine the ketchup, ginger, soy sauce and garlic; add the chicken. Seal bag and turn to coat; refrigerate for 15 minutes.

In a large nonstick skillet or wok, stir-fry peppers and onions in 1 teaspoon canola oil and 1 teaspoon sesame oil until crisp-tender. Remove the vegetables with a slotted spoon and keep warm.

In the same skillet, stir-fry chicken and marinade in remaining oil for 3-4 minutes or until no longer pink. Return vegetables to the pan; heat through. Serve with rice if desired. **Yield:** 3 servings.

Nutritional Analysis: One serving (1 cup chicken mixture, calculated without rice) equals 234 calories, 8 g fat (1 g saturated fat), 66 mg cholesterol, 496 mg

until well coated. In a skillet, brown chicken in butter over medium heat. Remove the chicken; set it aside and keep warm.

In the pan drippings, saute onion, green pepper and garlic until tender. Add pimientos and rice. Reduce heat; cook for 2 minutes, stirring occasionally. Stir in broth, turmeric, chili powder and remaining salt; bring to a boil. Pour into an ungreased 2-qt. baking dish; top with chicken.

Cover and bake at 350° for 45 minutes or until chicken juices run clear and rice is tender. **Yield:** 2 servings.

Apple Swiss Chicken

(Pictured at right)

Lynne Glashoerster, Edmonton, Alberta

My mom and I both like to experiment with recipes and created this about 50 years ago. It has come to the rescue for many impromptu occasions when I've had to adjust the serving sizes to unexpected numbers.

>   2 boneless skinless chicken breast halves
>   1/2 teaspoon dried rosemary, crushed
>   2 thin slices fully cooked ham
>   1 medium tart apple, peeled and thinly sliced,
>   *divided*
>   1 tablespoon vegetable oil
>   2 thin slices Swiss cheese
>   1 tablespoon apple juice *or* chicken broth
> Paprika

Flatten chicken breasts to 1/4-in. thickness; rub with rosemary. Top each with a ham slice and a few apple slices; roll up tightly. Secure with toothpicks. Place in a greased 1-qt. baking dish. Drizzle with the oil.

Bake, uncovered, at 350° for 20 minutes. Top with cheese and remaining apple slices; drizzle with apple juice. Sprinkle with paprika. Bake 10-15 minutes longer or until chicken juices run clear and cheese is melted. Discard toothpicks. **Yield:** 2 servings.

Asparagus, Apple and Chicken Salad

Nancy Horsburgh, Everett, Ontario

This cool, colorful salad is a palate-pleaser. Apples and asparagus seem an unlikely match, but they form a terrific trio with chicken! I make this salad often when asparagus is in season.

>   1 cup cut fresh asparagus (1-inch pieces)
>   2 tablespoons cider vinegar

>   2 tablespoons vegetable oil
>   2 teaspoons honey
>   2 teaspoons minced fresh parsley
>   1/2 teaspoon salt
>   1/4 teaspoon pepper
>   1 cup cubed cooked chicken
>   1/2 cup diced red apple
>   2 cups torn mixed greens
> Alfalfa sprouts, optional

Cook asparagus in a small amount of water until it is crisp-tender, about 3-4 minutes; drain and cool.

In a bowl, combine the vinegar, oil, honey, parsley, salt and pepper. Stir in the chicken, apple and asparagus; toss. Serve over greens. Garnish with alfalfa sprouts if desired. **Yield:** 3 servings.

Adjusting Recipes for Two

You can still cook wonderful meals for two by adjusting many of your favorite homemade recipes. Start with the recipes that yield between 4 and 6 servings; recipes or ingredients can be more easily divided by 2, 3 or 4.

When scaling down seasonings, such as herbs, salt, pepper or spices, begin by rounding off to the next smallest measurement. You can always add more seasoning to taste.

Pineapple Macadamia Chicken

(Pictured at right)

Kimberly Smith, Coeur d'Alene, Ohio

My family enjoys this summertime entree. It's quick, easy and oh-so-good served with cantaloupe wedges and iced tea. Each spicy-sweet bite reminds us of our trip to Hawaii.

 2 boneless skinless chicken breast halves
3/4 cup finely chopped macadamia nuts
1/4 teaspoon seasoned salt
1/4 teaspoon Caribbean jerk seasoning
1/8 teaspoon dried minced onion
1/8 teaspoon onion powder
1/8 teaspoon pepper
 1 egg, lightly beaten
 2 tablespoons vegetable oil
1/4 cup crushed pineapple
 1 tablespoon apricot preserves, warmed
Lettuce leaves

Flatten chicken to 1/4-in. thickness. In a shallow bowl, combine the nuts, seasoned salt, jerk seasoning, minced onion, onion powder and pepper.

Place the egg in another shallow bowl. Dip the chicken in egg; then coat with nut mixture. Let stand for 5 minutes.

In a skillet, cook chicken in oil for 3-4 minutes on each side or until chicken juices run clear. In a small bowl, combine pineapple and apricot preserves. Place lettuce on each plate; top with chicken and pineapple mixture. **Yield:** 2 servings.

Chicken Vegetable Soup

(Pictured below left)

Ruth Wimmer, Bland, Virginia

I love eating a big bowl of this colorful and fresh-tasting soup on a late summer or fall day. With the combination of veggies and chicken, it's such a great way to warm up!

 2 cups chicken broth
 1 cup fresh *or* frozen corn
 1 small celery rib, chopped
 1 small carrot, chopped
 1 small onion, chopped
 1 cup cubed cooked chicken
1/2 cup canned diced tomatoes
Salt and pepper to taste

In a saucepan, combine the broth, corn, celery, carrot and onion. Bring to a boil. Reduce the heat; cover and simmer for 25-30 minutes or until the vegetables are tender. Stir in the cooked chicken, tomatoes, salt and pepper; heat through. **Yield:** 2 servings.

Chicken 'n' Carrot Dumpling Stew

Ruth Haight, Markham, Ontario

It's been many years since I clipped this recipe from a magazine. It's always welcome at a family get-together.

1/2 pound boneless skinless chicken breasts
 1 cup chicken broth
 1 small onion, chopped

    1 celery rib, sliced
1/8 to 1/4 teaspoon salt
Dash dried thyme
Dash pepper
4-1/2 teaspoons all-purpose flour
    3 tablespoons water
DUMPLINGS:
1/2 cup all-purpose flour
    1 teaspoon baking powder
1/4 teaspoon salt
    2 tablespoons shortening
1/4 cup milk
    2 tablespoons finely grated carrot
1/2 teaspoon minced fresh parsley

In a large saucepan, combine the chicken, broth, onion, celery, salt, thyme and pepper. Bring to a boil. Reduce heat; cover and simmer for 15 minutes or until chicken juices run clear and vegetables are tender. Combine flour and water until smooth. Stir into broth. Bring to a boil; cook and stir for 1 minute or until thickened.

For dumplings, in a bowl, combine the flour, baking powder and salt; cut in shortening until mixture resembles coarse crumbs. Stir in the milk, carrot and parsley.

Drop by rounded tablespoonfuls into simmering broth. Cover and simmer for 20 minutes or until a toothpick inserted in a dumpling comes out clean (do not lift the cover while simmering). **Yield:** 2 servings.

Stuffed Chicken Breasts

Katherine Suter, Prescott, Arizona

This moist chicken with its savory filling makes a special entree for two, yet it's not tricky to prepare. The combination of apple, ham and chicken is wonderful.

3/4 cup chopped tart apple
1/2 cup finely chopped fully cooked ham
1/4 cup chopped fresh mushrooms
1/4 cup chopped red onion
    2 tablespoons vegetable oil, *divided*
    2 tablespoons Dijon mustard
1/3 cup dry bread crumbs
1/4 teaspoon lemon-pepper seasoning
    2 large boneless skinless chicken breast halves
    2 tablespoons all-purpose flour

In a small saucepan, saute the apple, ham, mushrooms and onion in 1 tablespoon oil until onion and apple are tender. Stir in mustard, bread crumbs and lemon-pepper. Flatten chicken breasts to 1/4-in. thickness; top each with the apple mixture. Roll up and secure with toothpicks. Coat with flour.

In a skillet, brown chicken in remaining oil. Place in an 8-in. square baking dish. Bake, uncovered, at 350° for 20-30 minutes or until juices run clear. Discard toothpicks. **Yield:** 2 servings.

Sourdough Chicken Sandwiches

(Pictured below)

Joe Urban, West Chicago, Illinois

My family loves chicken, so I came up with this easy sandwich recipe. The chicken stays moist and tasty prepared this way. With potatoes or fries and a salad, it's a complete meal.

    2 boneless skinless chicken breast halves
    1 egg, beaten
1/2 cup seasoned bread crumbs
    2 tablespoons butter
    4 slices sourdough bread
    2 to 3 teaspoons mayonnaise
    2 lettuce leaves
    2 Swiss cheese slices
    2 tomato slices
    2 bacon strips, cooked

Pound chicken to 1/4-in. thickness. Dip chicken in egg, then coat with crumbs. In a skillet over medium-high heat, cook chicken in butter on both sides until juices run clear, about 8 minutes.

Spread bread with mayonnaise. Top two slices with lettuce, cheese, tomato, bacon and chicken. Top with remaining bread. **Yield:** 2 servings.

Greek Chicken Dinner

(Pictured below)

Mary Anne Janzen, Kilarney, Manitoba

I received this wonderful recipe from our daughter-in-law, who is from Athens, Greece.

- 1 to 1-1/4 pounds meaty bone-in chicken pieces
- 2 to 3 tablespoons olive oil, *divided*
- 2 medium carrots, cut into 1-inch pieces
- 1 medium potato, cut into 1/2-inch cubes
- 1 small onion, quartered
- 1 teaspoon minced fresh parsley
- 1 teaspoon dried basil
- 1/4 teaspoon dried oregano
- 1/8 teaspoon garlic powder
- Salt and pepper to taste
- 1 to 2 tablespoons lemon juice

In a skillet, brown chicken in 1 tablespoon oil. In a greased 9-in. square baking dish, place the carrots, potato and onion. Drizzle with remaining oil and toss to coat. Top with chicken.

In a small bowl, combine the parsley, basil, oregano, garlic powder, salt and pepper. Sprinkle over chicken and vegetables, then sprinkle with lemon juice.

Cover and bake at 375° for 40 minutes. Uncover; bake 15-20 minutes longer or until chicken juices run clear and vegetables are tender. **Yield:** 2-3 servings.

Basil Chicken Strips

Barbara Rokow, Geneva, New York

This easy chicken entree seasoned with basil is great for the weeknight rush. I like to serve it with broccoli and Parmesan noodles.

- 1/2 pound boneless skinless chicken breasts, cut into strips
- 2 tablespoons all-purpose flour
- 3 tablespoons butter
- 2 tablespoons red wine vinegar
- 1/2 teaspoon dried basil

In a large resealable plastic bag, shake chicken strips and flour until coated. In a large skillet over medium-high heat, melt butter.

Add the chicken; saute for 5 minutes. Stir in the vinegar and basil; cook until the chicken juices run clear. **Yield:** 2 servings.

Hearty Chicken Club

(Pictured at right)

Debbie Johanesen, Missoula, Montana

I discovered the recipe for this sizable sandwich a while back and modified it to suit my family's tastes. We love it...the only problem is trying to open wide enough to take a bite!

- 1/4 cup mayonnaise
- 2 tablespoons salsa
- 4 slices seven-grain sandwich bread
- 2 lettuce leaves
- 4 slices tomato
- 8 ounces sliced cooked chicken *or* turkey
- 4 bacon strips, cooked
- 4 slices cheddar cheese
- 1 ripe avocado, sliced

Combine mayonnaise and salsa; spread on two slices of bread. Layer with lettuce, tomato, chicken or turkey, bacon, cheese and avocado. Top with remaining bread. **Yield:** 2 servings.

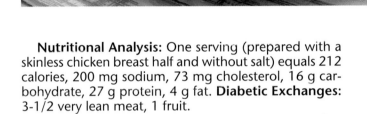

Apricot Chicken

Winifred Brown, Jamesburg, New Jersey

I've fixed this tender glazed chicken for myself on many special occasions. It looks as good as it tastes.

✓ Uses less fat, sugar or salt. Includes Nutritional Analysis and Diabetic Exchanges.

- 2 tablespoons apricot preserves
- 2 tablespoons reduced-fat French salad dressing

Pinch ginger, optional

- 2 bone-in chicken breast halves

Salt and pepper to taste

In a small bowl, combine the apricot preserves, salad dressing and ginger if desired and set the mixture aside.

Place chicken in a greased 8-in. square baking pan; sprinkle with salt and pepper. Top with apricot mixture. Bake, uncovered, at 350° for 50-55 minutes or until chicken juices run clear. **Yield:** 2 servings.

Timely Tip

Use frozen chopped onions when a recipe calls for a small amount of onion (such as 1 or 2 tablespoons). It saves time and eliminates leftover onion!

Nutritional Analysis: One serving (prepared with a skinless chicken breast half and without salt) equals 212 calories, 200 mg sodium, 73 mg cholesterol, 16 g carbohydrate, 27 g protein, 4 g fat. **Diabetic Exchanges:** 3-1/2 very lean meat, 1 fruit.

Crispy Dijon Chicken

Ella West, Lake Charles, Louisiana

You and your dinner partner are sure to relish this doubly delicious dish. Yogurt, lemon juice and Dijon mustard give oven-baked chicken a tangy taste, while cornflake crumbs provide plenty of crunch.

- 1/4 cup plain yogurt
- 1/2 teaspoon salt-free herb seasoning blend
- 1/2 teaspoon lemon juice
- 1/2 teaspoon Dijon mustard
- 1/2 cup cornflake crumbs
- 1/4 cup grated Parmesan cheese
- 2 bone-in chicken breast halves

In a shallow bowl, combine yogurt, seasoning blend, lemon juice and mustard. In another bowl, combine the cornflake crumbs and Parmesan cheese.

Roll the chicken in yogurt mixture, then in crumb mixture. Place in a greased 8-in. square baking pan. Bake, uncovered, at 350° for 35-45 minutes or until juices run clear. **Yield:** 2 servings.

6 Oven Entrees

Chicken Rice Burritos

(Pictured at left)

Suzanne Adams, Laguna Niguel, California

For a nice alternative to beef and bean burritos, I use this recipe, which I discovered several years back. If I fix the chicken mixture the night before, the next day's dinner is a snap.

- 1/3 cup sliced green onions
- 1 garlic clove, minced
- 2 tablespoons butter
- 7 cups shredded cooked chicken
- 1 tablespoon chili powder
- 2-1/2 cups chicken broth, *divided*
- 1 jar (16 ounces) picante sauce, *divided*
- 1 cup uncooked long grain rice
- 1/2 cup sliced ripe olives
- 3 cups (12 ounces) shredded cheddar cheese, *divided*
- 12 flour tortillas (10 inches), warmed
- Additional picante sauce and cheddar cheese

In a skillet, saute onions and garlic in butter until tender. Stir in chicken, chili powder, 1/4 cup broth and 3/4 cup of picante sauce. Heat through and set aside.

In a medium saucepan, bring rice and remaining broth to a boil. Reduce heat; cover and simmer 20 minutes. Stir in remaining picante sauce; cover and simmer 5-10 minutes or until rice is tender. Stir into chicken mixture. Add olives and 2 cups cheese.

Spoon 1 cup filling, off center, on each tortilla. Fold sides and ends over filling, then roll up. Arrange burritos in two ungreased 13-in. x 9-in. x 2-in. baking dishes. Sprinkle with the remaining cheese.

Cover and bake at 375° for 10-15 minutes or until heated through. Garnish with picante sauce and cheese. **Yield:** 6 servings.

Chicken Rosemary

Emily Chaney, Penobscot, Maine

It doesn't take a lot of rosemary to give your dishes wonderful flavor. It's especially tasty in this chicken dish, which also gets a little zip from Dijon mustard.

- 4 boneless skinless chicken breast halves
- 2 to 3 tablespoons Dijon mustard
- 1/2 teaspoon garlic powder
- 2 tablespoons minced fresh rosemary *or 2 teaspoons dried rosemary, crushed*
- Pepper to taste
- 1/2 cup grated Parmesan cheese

Place chicken in a greased 11-in. x 7-in. x 2-in. baking dish. Combine mustard and garlic powder; spread over the chicken. Sprinkle with rosemary and pepper. Top with cheese.

Bake, uncovered, at 350° for 45 minutes or until juices run clear. **Yield:** 4 servings.

Sage Chicken Cordon Bleu

Martha Stine, Johnstown, Pennsylvania

It's nice to surprise the family with special meals like this during the week. I usually double the recipe so we can enjoy leftovers the next day.

- 6 boneless skinless chicken breast halves
- 6 slices thinly sliced deli ham
- 6 strips mozzarella cheese (3 inches x 1-1/2 inches x 1/2 inch)
- 1 medium tomato, seeded and chopped
- 3/4 teaspoon dried sage leaves
- 1/3 cup dry bread crumbs
- 2 tablespoons grated Parmesan cheese
- 2 tablespoons minced fresh parsley
- 1/4 cup butter, melted

Flatten chicken to 1/8-in. thickness. Place a ham slice, a mozzarella cheese strip, 1 tablespoon tomato and 1/8 teaspoon sage down the center of each chicken breast. Roll up and tuck in ends; secure with toothpicks.

In a shallow bowl, combine bread crumbs, Parmesan cheese and parsley. Dip chicken in butter, then roll in crumb mixture. Place in a greased 9-in. square baking dish. Drizzle with remaining butter.

Bake, uncovered, at 350° for 45 minutes or until chicken juices run clear. Discard toothpicks. **Yield:** 6 servings.

Apple Stuffed Chicken

(Pictured above)

Joan Wrigley, Lynden, Washington

A friend served this wonderful stuffed chicken when we were over for dinner, and we enjoyed it so much I asked for the recipe.

   1 package (6 ounces) chicken-flavored
      stuffing mix
   1 broiler/fryer chicken (about 3-1/2 pounds)
1/2 teaspoon salt
1/4 teaspoon pepper
   1 tablespoon vegetable oil
   1 cup chopped peeled apple
1/4 cup chopped celery
1/4 cup chopped walnuts
1/4 cup raisins
1/2 teaspoon grated lemon peel
GLAZE:
1/2 cup apple jelly
   1 tablespoon lemon juice
1/2 teaspoon ground cinnamon

Prepare stuffing according to package directions. Meanwhile, sprinkle inside of chicken with salt and pepper; rub outside with oil. In a large bowl, mix stuffing with apple, celery, nuts, raisins and lemon peel. Lightly stuff chicken. Place with breast side up on a rack in a shallow roasting pan.

Bake, uncovered, at 350° for 1 hour. In a saucepan, combine glaze ingredients; simmer 3 minutes. Brush over chicken. Bake 20-30 minutes longer or until chicken juices run clear, brushing occasionally with glaze. **Yield:** 4-6 servings.

Asparagus Chicken Divan

Jeanne Koelsch, San Rafael, California

I first came across this recipe at a restaurant while living in New York City many years ago. This makes a delectable dish for lunch or dinner served with a simple tossed green salad.

1 pound boneless skinless chicken breasts
2 pounds fresh asparagus, trimmed
1 can (10-3/4 ounces) condensed cream of
    chicken soup, undiluted
1 teaspoon Worcestershire sauce
1/4 teaspoon ground nutmeg
1 cup grated Parmesan cheese, *divided*
1/2 cup heavy whipping cream, whipped
3/4 cup mayonnaise

Broil chicken 6 in. from the heat until juices run clear. Meanwhile, in a large skillet, bring 1/2 in. of water to a boil. Add asparagus. Reduce heat; cover and simmer for 3-5 minutes or until crisp-tender. Drain and place in a greased shallow 2-1/2-qt. baking dish. Cut chicken into thin slices.

In a bowl, combine the soup, Worcestershire sauce and nutmeg. Spread half over asparagus. Sprinkle with 1/3 cup Parmesan cheese. Top with chicken. Spread remaining soup mixture over chicken; sprinkle with 1/3 cup Parmesan cheese.

Bake, uncovered, at 400° for 20 minutes. Fold whipped cream into mayonnaise; spread over top. Sprinkle with remaining Parmesan cheese. Broil 4-6 in. from the heat for about 2 minutes or until golden brown. **Yield:** 6-8 servings.

Editor's Note: Reduced-fat or fat-free mayonnaise may not be substituted for regular mayonnaise in this recipe.

Greek Chicken

Nina Ivanoff, Prince George, British Columbia

This recipe earned me first place in a local cooking contest. For special occasions, I add four to six sun-dried tomatoes (soaked and drained according to package directions) to the cheese mixture before blending.

4 boneless skinless chicken breast halves
2 packages (4 ounces *each*) feta cheese
1 can (4-1/4 ounces) chopped ripe olives,
    drained
2 tablespoons olive oil, *divided*
1/2 teaspoon dried oregano
2 tablespoons dry white wine *or* chicken broth
1 teaspoon sugar
1 teaspoon balsamic vinegar
1 garlic clove, minced
1/4 teaspoon dried thyme
1 medium onion, sliced

Flatten chicken breasts to 1/8-in. thickness; set aside. In a food processor or blender, combine the cheese, olives, 1 tablespoon oil and oregano; cover and process until mixture reaches a thick chunky paste consistency. Spread over chicken breasts; roll up and tuck in ends. Secure with a wooden toothpick.

In a bowl, combine wine or broth, sugar, vinegar,

garlic, thyme and remaining oil. Pour into an ungreased 2-qt. baking dish. Top with onion. Place chicken over onion. Cover and bake at 350° for 30 minutes. Uncover and baste with pan juices. Bake 15-20 minutes longer or until chicken juices run clear. **Yield:** 4 servings.

Chicken French Bread Pizza

(Pictured below)

Laura Mahaffey, Annapolis, Maryland

This delicious recipe is great for casual get-togethers. It's easy, too, since it uses convenient chunk chicken. With the great combination of cheeses and veggies, it's always gobbled up quickly at my house.

1 loaf (1 pound) French bread
1/2 cup butter, softened
1/2 cup shredded cheddar cheese
1/3 cup grated Parmesan cheese
1 garlic clove, minced
1/4 teaspoon Italian seasoning
1 can (10 ounces) chunk white chicken,
    drained and flaked
1 cup (4 ounces) shredded mozzarella cheese
1/2 cup chopped sweet red pepper
1/2 cup chopped green onions

Cut bread in half lengthwise, then in half widthwise. Combine the butter, cheddar, Parmesan, garlic and Italian seasoning; spread over bread. Top with the remaining ingredients. Place on a baking sheet.

Bake at 350° for 10-12 minutes or until cheeses are melted. Cut into smaller pieces if desired. **Yield:** 4 servings.

Bring to a boil; cook and stir for 2 minutes or until thickened. Add chicken. Cover and bake at 350° for 45-50 minutes.

Increase heat to 425°. For dumplings, combine the flour, baking powder and salt in a bowl; cut in butter until crumbly. Combine the egg and milk; stir into dry ingredients just until moistened. Drop batter into 12 mounds onto hot broth.

Bake, uncovered, at 425° for 10 minutes. Cover and bake 10 minutes longer or until a toothpick inserted into a dumpling comes out clean. **Yield:** 4 servings.

Baked Chicken

(Pictured below)

Barbara Wheeler, Sparks Glencoe, Maryland

A tangy from-scratch sauce makes this tender chicken extra flavorful. My mom is an excellent cook who has fixed delicious dishes like this one for years. If you're in a hurry, just prepare it ahead and pop it in the oven when you get home after a busy day.

   1 broiler/fryer chicken (3 pounds), cut up
   1 tablespoon all-purpose flour
1/4 cup water

Apple Cider Chicken 'n' Dumplings

(Pictured above)

Margaret Sumner-Wichmann
Questa, New Mexico

I came up with this recipe one fall when I had an abundance of apple cider. Adding some to a down-home classic was a delectable decision. Now my family asks for this dish often!

   8 chicken thighs (about 3 pounds), skin removed
   2 tablespoons butter
   1 medium red onion, chopped
   1 celery rib, chopped
   2 tablespoons minced fresh parsley
Salt and pepper to taste
   3 tablespoons all-purpose flour
   3 cups chicken broth
   1 cup apple cider *or* apple juice
DUMPLINGS:
   2 cups all-purpose flour
   1 tablespoon baking powder
1/2 teaspoon salt
   1 tablespoon cold butter
   1 egg, lightly beaten
2/3 cup milk

In a Dutch oven, brown chicken in butter; remove and set aside. In the same pan, combine the onion, celery, parsley, salt and pepper; cook and stir until vegetables are tender. Sprinkle with flour and mix well. Add broth and cider.

1/4 cup packed brown sugar
1/4 cup ketchup
2 tablespoons white vinegar
2 tablespoons lemon juice
2 tablespoons Worcestershire sauce
1 small onion, chopped
1 teaspoon ground mustard
1 teaspoon paprika
1 teaspoon chili powder
1/2 teaspoon salt
1/8 teaspoon pepper

Place chicken in a greased 13-in. x 9-in. x 2-in. baking dish. In a saucepan, whisk flour and water until smooth. Stir in brown sugar, ketchup, vinegar, lemon juice and Worcestershire sauce. Bring to a boil; cook and stir for 2 minutes or until thickened. Cool.

Stir in the remaining ingredients. Pour over chicken. Cover and refrigerate for 2-4 hours. Remove from the refrigerator 30 minutes before baking. Bake, uncovered, at 350° for 35-45 minutes or until chicken juices run clear. **Yield:** 4 servings.

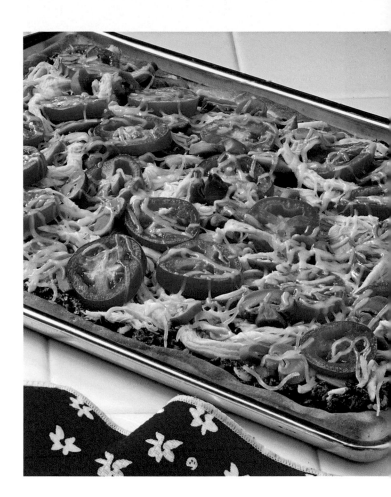

Chicken Pesto Pan Pizza

(Pictured at right)

Juanita Fleck, Bullhead City, Arizona

A packaged pesto mix tastefully replaces traditional tomato sauce in this tempting pizza. Served alongside a tossed green salad, this is one of my husband's favorite meals.

1 tube (10 ounces) refrigerated pizza crust
1/2 cup water
3 tablespoons olive oil
1 envelope pesto sauce mix
1 package (10 ounces) frozen chopped spinach, thawed and squeezed dry
1/2 cup ricotta cheese
1/4 cup chopped onion
2 cups shredded cooked chicken
1 jar (4-1/2 ounces) sliced mushrooms, drained
4 plum tomatoes, sliced
1 cup (4 ounces) shredded Swiss cheese
1/4 cup grated Romano cheese

Unroll pizza crust into an ungreased 15-in. x 10-in. x 1-in. baking pan; flatten dough and build up edges slightly. Prick dough several times with a fork. Bake at 425° for 7 minutes or until lightly browned.

Meanwhile, combine the water, oil and pesto sauce mix in a saucepan. Cook until heated through (do not boil). Add the spinach, ricotta and onion; mix well. Spread over crust.

Top with the chicken, mushrooms, tomatoes and Swiss and Romano cheeses. Bake at 425° for 7 minutes or until the crust is golden and the cheese is melted. **Yield:** 6-8 servings.

Chicken in Plum Sauce

Patricia Collins, Imbler, Oregon

Honey, plums and garlic combine in the sauce for a mouth-watering main dish. The plums I use grow wild in the mountains near our home. But canned plums work just as well.

1 broiler/fryer chicken (3-1/2 to 4 pounds), cut up
3/4 cup all-purpose flour
3 tablespoons vegetable oil
2 cans (16-1/2 ounces *each*) whole plums, pitted
1/2 cup honey
1 tablespoon vinegar
1 to 2 garlic cloves, minced

Coat chicken pieces with flour; brown in oil in a large skillet over medium heat. Transfer to a greased 13-in. x 9-in. x 2-in. baking pan.

Drain plums, reserving syrup; remove pits and coarsely chop plums in a food processor. Pour into a measuring cup; add enough syrup to equal 2 cups. Place in a saucepan. Add honey, vinegar and garlic; bring to a boil. Cook and stir for 2 minutes. Pour over chicken.

Bake, uncovered, at 350° for 45 minutes or until chicken juices run clear. **Yield:** 4-6 servings.

Chicken Parmigiana

(Pictured above)

Rhonda Schiel, Magnolia, Texas

A nicely seasoned breading coats the tender chicken breasts in this attractive entree. When I have extra time, I make my own herbed tomato sauce instead of using prepared spaghetti sauce.

> ✓ Uses less fat, sugar or salt. Includes Nutritional Analysis and Diabetic Exchanges.

- 1/2 cup dry bread crumbs
- 3 tablespoons grated Parmesan cheese
- 3/4 teaspoon Italian seasoning
- 1/2 teaspoon garlic powder
- 1/2 teaspoon salt
- 1/4 cup egg substitute
- 4 boneless skinless chicken breast halves (1 pound)
- 1 jar (26 ounces) meatless spaghetti sauce
- 3/4 cup shredded part-skim mozzarella cheese
- 1/4 cup shredded Parmesan cheese

In a shallow bowl, combine the bread crumbs, grated Parmesan cheese, Italian seasoning, garlic powder and salt. In another bowl, beat egg substitute. Dip chicken in egg substitute, then roll in crumbs.

Place in a 13-in. x 9-in. x 2-in. baking dish coated with nonstick cooking spray. Bake, uncovered, at 375° for 10 minutes. Turn chicken; bake for 10 minutes. Pour spaghetti sauce over chicken; bake for 5 minutes. Sprinkle with cheeses; bake 10 minutes longer or until chicken juices run clear. **Yield:** 4 servings.

Nutritional Analysis: One serving equals 412 calories, 15 g fat (5 g saturated fat), 88 mg cholesterol, 1,420 mg sodium, 32 g carbohydrate, 5 g fiber, 37 g protein. **Diabetic Exchanges:** 4 lean meat, 2 starch, 1/2 fat.

No-Fuss Chicken

Marilyn Dick, Centralia, Missouri

This recipe could hardly be simpler to prepare. The chicken gets a wonderful tangy taste, and no one will know you used convenient ingredients like a bottle of salad dressing and onion soup mix…unless you tell them!

- 1 bottle (16 ounces) Russian *or* Catalina salad dressing
- 2/3 cup apricot preserves
- 2 envelopes dry onion soup mix
- 16 boneless skinless chicken breast halves

Hot cooked rice

In a bowl, combine dressing, preserves and soup mix. Place chicken in two ungreased 11-in. x 7-in. x 2-in. baking pans; top with dressing mixture. Cover and bake at 350° for 20 minutes; baste. Bake, uncovered, 20 minutes longer or until chicken juices run clear. Serve over rice. **Yield:** 16 servings.

Chicken Supreme

Marlene Nutter, Thedford, Nebraska

Strips of Monterey Jack cheese tucked inside chicken make this entree extra special. Crushed Caesar salad croutons are a unique addition to the coating.

- 4 ounces Monterey Jack cheese
- 1/2 cup butter, softened

Pounding Chicken

Recipes, such as Chicken Supreme on this page, call for flattened or pounded chicken. In order to give pieces of chicken an even thickness, follow these steps:

1. Place the boneless chicken breast between two pieces of waxed paper.
2. Starting in the center and working out to the edges, pound lightly with a meat mallet's flat side until the chicken is even in thickness.

1 teaspoon minced fresh parsley
  1 teaspoon dried oregano
1/2 to 1 teaspoon dried marjoram
  8 boneless skinless chicken breast halves
    (about 3 pounds)
1/2 teaspoon seasoned salt
1/2 cup all-purpose flour
  2 eggs, beaten
1-3/4 cups crushed Caesar salad croutons
1/2 cup white wine *or* chicken broth

Cut the Monterey Jack cheese into eight 2-1/4-in. x 1-in. x 3/8-in. strips. In a bowl, combine the softened butter, parsley, oregano and marjoram; spread 1-1/2 teaspoons over each cheese strip. Cover and refrigerate the cheese and remaining butter mixture for at least 2 hours.

Flatten chicken to 1/8-in. thickness; sprinkle with seasoned salt. Place a cheese strip on each piece of chicken. Roll up and tuck in ends; secure with a toothpick. Coat chicken on all sides with flour. Dip in eggs, then coat with croutons.

Place seam side down in a greased 13-in. x 9-in. x 2-in. baking dish. Bake, uncovered, at 350° for 30 minutes. In a saucepan, combine wine or broth and reserved butter mixture; heat until butter is melted. Pour over chicken. Bake 20-25 minutes longer or until chicken juices run clear. Discard toothpicks before serving. **Yield:** 8 servings.

Cranberry Chicken

(Pictured below)

Linda Rock, Stratford, Wisconsin

Tender baked chicken gets dressed up for any occasion with a chunky spiced fruit sauce.

✓ Uses less fat, sugar or salt. Includes Nutritional Analysis and Diabetic Exchanges.

  6 boneless skinless chicken breast halves
    (1-1/2 pounds)
  1 can (16 ounces) whole-berry cranberry
    sauce
  1 large tart apple, peeled and chopped
1/2 cup raisins
1/4 cup chopped walnuts
  1 teaspoon curry powder

Place chicken in a 13-in. x 9-in. x 2-in. baking dish coated with nonstick cooking spray. Bake, uncovered, at 350° for 20 minutes. Meanwhile, combine the remaining ingredients. Spoon over chicken. Bake, uncovered, 20-25 minutes longer or until chicken juices run clear. **Yield:** 6 servings.

Nutritional Analysis: One serving equals 334 calories, 81 mg sodium, 73 mg cholesterol, 42 g carbohydrate, 28 g protein, 6 g fat, 2 g fiber. **Diabetic Exchanges:** 4 very lean meat, 3 fruit.

Oven-Fried Chicken

(Pictured below)

Suzanne McKinley, Lyons, Georgia

My mother, who is diabetic, often relies on this recipe. The meat is lightly seasoned and stays moist.

✓ Uses less fat, sugar or salt. Includes Nutritional Analysis and Diabetic Exchanges.

1-1/2 **cups instant nonfat dry milk powder**
   1 **tablespoon paprika**
   2 **teaspoons poultry seasoning**
1/4 **teaspoon pepper**
   4 **boneless skinless chicken breast halves**
     (1 pound)

Combine the first four ingredients in a large resealable plastic bag. Add chicken, one piece at a time, and shake to coat. Place in an 8-in. square baking pan that has been coated with nonstick cooking spray. Bake, uncovered, at 350° for 30 minutes or until juices run clear. **Yield:** 4 servings.
  Nutritional Analysis: One serving equals 240 calories, 204 mg sodium, 78 mg cholesterol, 15 g carbohydrate, 36 g protein, 4 g fat. **Diabetic Exchanges:** 4 very lean meat, 1 starch.

Zesty Chicken Wings

Joan Rose, Langley, British Columbia

These spicy barbecue wings are so easy to make. I fix a double batch since my family thinks they're great. You should see them disappear!

1/2 **cup corn syrup**
1/2 **cup ketchup**
1/4 **cup cider vinegar**
1/4 **cup Worcestershire sauce**
1/4 **cup Dijon mustard**
   1 **small onion, chopped**
   3 **garlic cloves, minced**
   1 **tablespoon chili powder**
 16 **whole chicken wings (about 3 pounds)**

In a saucepan, combine the first eight ingredients. Bring to a boil. Reduce heat; simmer, uncovered, for 15-20 minutes or until thickened. Meanwhile, cut chicken wings into three sections; discard wing tips. Place wings in a well-greased 15-in. x 10-in. x 1-in. baking pan.
  Bake at 375° for 30 minutes, turning once. Brush with sauce. Bake 20-25 minutes longer, turning and basting once, or until the chicken juices run clear. **Yield:** 10-12 servings.

Crunchy Baked Chicken

(Pictured above right)

Essie Malatt, Converse, Indiana

One bite of tender chicken in a crunchy golden coating explains why I give this recipe such a workout. Besides serving it at home for the two of us, I make a big batch for our senior group at church.

✓ Uses less fat, sugar or salt. Includes Nutritional Analysis and Diabetic Exchanges.

3/4 **cup fat-free Western salad dressing**
1/2 **teaspoon chili powder**

 4 boneless skinless chicken breast halves (1 pound)
 20 fresh asparagus spears (about 1 pound), trimmed
4-1/2 teaspoons canola oil
 2 teaspoons lemon juice
 1/2 teaspoon dried basil
 1/4 teaspoon dried thyme
 1/4 teaspoon pepper
 1/8 teaspoon salt
 1/4 cup chopped green onions
 2 teaspoons cornstarch
 1 cup chicken broth

Flatten chicken breasts slightly. Wrap each around five asparagus spears; secure with toothpicks. Place in a 13-in. x 9-in. x 2-in. baking dish coated with nonstick cooking spray. Combine oil, lemon juice and seasonings; pour over bundles. Cover asparagus tips with foil.

Cover and bake at 350° for 15 minutes. Uncover; sprinkle with onions. Bake 12-15 minutes longer or until chicken juices run clear and asparagus is crisp-tender. Remove bundles to a serving platter; keep warm.

In a saucepan, combine cornstarch and broth until smooth; stir in pan juices. Bring to a boil; cook and stir for 2 minutes or until thickened. Remove toothpicks from bundles; top with sauce. **Yield:** 4 servings.

Nutritional Analysis: One serving (1 bundle with about 1/3 cup sauce) equals 207 calories, 7 g fat (1 g saturated fat), 66 mg cholesterol, 316 mg sodium, 6 g carbohydrate, 2 g fiber, 29 g protein. **Diabetic Exchanges:** 3 lean meat, 1 vegetable, 1 fat.

 1/4 teaspoon salt
 8 bone-in chicken breast halves (10 ounces *each*), skin removed
2-1/2 cups crushed cornflakes
DIPPING SAUCE (not shown):
 1/4 cup chopped green pepper
 1/4 cup chopped onion
 3/4 cup fat-free Western salad dressing
 1/2 teaspoon chili powder
 1/4 teaspoon salt

In a shallow bowl, combine salad dressing, chili powder and salt. Dip chicken in mixture, then roll in cornflakes. Place in a 15-in. x 10-in. x 1-in. baking pan coated with nonstick cooking spray. Bake, uncovered, at 350° for 35-40 minutes or until chicken juices run clear.

Meanwhile, for sauce, combine green pepper and onion in a microwave-safe bowl. Microwave on high for 1-1/2 minutes. Stir in remaining ingredients. Cover and cook 30-60 seconds longer or until heated through. Serve with chicken. **Yield:** 8 servings.

Nutritional Analysis: One serving (1 chicken breast half with 2 tablespoons sauce) equals 278 calories, 1 g fat (trace saturated fat), 66 mg cholesterol, 888 mg sodium, 38 g carbohydrate, 1 g fiber, 29 g protein. **Diabetic Exchanges:** 3-1/2 lean meat, 1 starch.

Chicken and Asparagus Bundles

(Pictured at right)

Donna Lohnes, Wooster, Ohio

Asparagus is a mainstay when I want something unusual but simple for guests. For variety, you can leave off the sauce and serve the bundles chilled for a delicious lunch.

Microwave Directions: (timing based on a 700-watt oven): Place chicken in a greased glass pie plate. Microwave on high for 4 minutes. Turn plate; microwave for 3-4 minutes or until juices run clear. Let stand 5 minutes. **Yield:** 6 servings.

Nacho Chicken

Thom Britton, Three Rivers, Michigan

I have been serving this rich and zippy chicken dish for several years, and it's a favorite of my family and friends. It's sure to disappear quickly at potluck suppers, too.

> 4 cups cubed cooked chicken
> 1 pound process cheese (Velveeta), cubed
> 2 cans (10-3/4 ounces *each*) condensed cream of chicken soup, undiluted
> 1 can (10 ounces) diced tomatoes and green chilies, undrained
> 1 cup chopped onion
> 1/2 teaspoon garlic salt
> 1/4 teaspoon pepper
> 1 package (14-1/2 ounces) nacho cheese tortilla chips

In a large bowl, combine the first seven ingredients; mix well. Crush chips; set aside 1 cup for topping. Add remaining chips to chicken mixture. Spoon into a greased 13-in. x 9-in. x 2-in. baking dish; sprinkle with reserved chips.

Bake, uncovered, at 350° for 30 minutes or until cheese is melted and edges are bubbly. **Yield:** 8-10 servings.

Chicken Kiev

(Pictured above)

Lynne Peterson, Salt Lake City, Utah

A favorite aunt shared this special recipe with me. It makes attractive individual servings fancy enough to be served for company. They have great flavor.

> 1/4 cup butter, softened
> 1 tablespoon grated onion
> 1 tablespoon chopped fresh parsley
> 1/2 teaspoon garlic powder
> 1/2 teaspoon dried tarragon
> 1/4 teaspoon pepper
> 6 boneless skinless chicken breast halves
> 1 egg
> 1 tablespoon milk
> 1 envelope (2-3/4 ounces) seasoned chicken coating mix

Combine the softened butter, grated onion, chopped parsley, garlic powder, tarragon and pepper. Shape mixture into six pencil-thin strips about 2 in. long; place on waxed paper. Freeze until firm, about 30 minutes.

Flatten each chicken breast to 1/4 in. Place one butter strip in the center of each chicken breast. Fold long sides over butter; fold ends up and secure with a toothpick.

In a bowl, beat egg and milk; place coating mix in another bowl. Dip chicken, then roll in coating mix. Place chicken, seam side down, in a greased 13-in. x 9-in. x 2-in. baking pan.

Bake, uncovered, at 425° for 35-40 minutes or until the chicken is no longer pink and juices run clear. Remove toothpicks before serving.

Onion-Topped Chicken

Kay Faust, Deerwood, Minnesota

I throw together this saucy combination of tender chicken and potatoes when family or friends come to visit. French-fried onions add golden crunch to the baked dish.

> 4 boneless skinless chicken breast halves
> 4 medium potatoes, peeled and halved
> 1 can (10-3/4 ounces) condensed cream of chicken soup, undiluted
> 1 cup (8 ounces) sour cream
> 1 can (2.8 ounces) french-fried onions

Place the chicken breast halves in a greased 9-in. square baking dish. Arrange potatoes around chicken. Combine the soup and sour cream; spread over chicken and potatoes.

Bake, uncovered, at 350° for 1-1/4 hours. Sprinkle with onions and bake 10 minutes longer or until juices run clear. **Yield:** 4 servings.

Spicy Hot Wings

(Pictured below)

Anna Free, Loudonville, Ohio

Friends and family go wild when I serve these tongue-tingling baked chicken wings. The creamy dipping sauce is a mild accompaniment that gets lip-smacking flavor from blue cheese.

> 10 whole chicken wings (about 2 pounds)
> 1/2 cup butter, melted
> 2 to 5 teaspoons hot pepper sauce
> 3/4 teaspoon garlic salt
> 1/4 teaspoon paprika
> **DIPPING SAUCE:**
> 3/4 cup sour cream
> 1 tablespoon dried minced onion
> 1 tablespoon milk
> 1/2 cup crumbled blue cheese
> 1/4 teaspoon garlic salt
> 1/8 teaspoon ground mustard
> **Paprika, optional**
> **Celery sticks, optional**

Cut chicken wings into three sections; discard wing tips. Place wings in a greased 15-in. x 10-in. x 1-in. baking pan. Combine butter, hot pepper sauce, garlic salt and paprika; pour over wings.

Bake at 375° for 30 minutes. Turn; bake 20-25 minutes longer or until chicken juices run clear.

Meanwhile, for sauce, combine the sour cream, onion, milk, cheese, garlic salt and mustard in a blender. Cover and process until smooth. Pour into a bowl; sprinkle with paprika if desired. Cover and refrigerate until serving.

Drain wings. Serve with sauce and celery if desired. **Yield:** 6-8 servings.

Hot Wing Hints

Chicken wings are great for snacks, appetizers and other menu options.

Often, recipes call for whole chicken wings. Then you need to cut the wings into three parts and discard the wing tips.

Instead of the whole chicken wings, you can substitute uncooked chicken wing sections in most recipes. Here are a few guidelines:
- 10 whole wings = 2 pounds wing sections.
- 12 whole wings = 2-1/2 pounds wing sections.
- 16 whole wings = 3 pounds wing sections.

In the same skillet, brown chicken, skin side down, in remaining oil. Turn chicken. Bake, uncovered, at 375° for 25-30 minutes or until chicken juices run clear. **Yield:** 4 servings.

Southwest Roll-Ups

(Pictured below)

Dean Schrock, Jacksonville, Florida

Taste buds tingle when I serve these tempting tortillas stuffed with a zesty mixture of chicken, refried beans, salsa and jalapeno peppers. It's a savory dish that makes any buffet a fiesta.

> 2 tablespoons salsa
> 1 to 2 jalapeno peppers, seeded
> 1 garlic clove
> 2 tablespoons chopped onion
> 1 can (16 ounces) refried beans
> 1/2 teaspoon ground cumin
> 1 tablespoon chopped fresh cilantro, optional
> 1 cup cubed cooked chicken
> 1 cup (4 ounces) shredded cheddar cheese, *divided*

Zucchini-Stuffed Chicken

(Pictured above)

Lynda Postnikoff, Beausejour, Manitoba

Now that we're empty nesters, my husband is the brave one who gets to test my new recipes. This one quickly received a thumbs-up.

> 1 medium onion, chopped
> 3 garlic cloves, minced
> 2 tablespoons olive oil, *divided*
> 2 cups diced zucchini
> 1 cup diced sweet red pepper
> 1/3 cup grated Parmesan cheese
> 1 tablespoon minced fresh basil *or* 1 teaspoon dried basil
> 1/2 teaspoon salt
> 1/4 teaspoon pepper
> 4 bone-in chicken breast halves with skin

In a large ovenproof skillet, saute onion and garlic in 1 tablespoon oil for 3 minutes. Add zucchini and red pepper; saute for 3 minutes. Remove from the heat; stir in Parmesan cheese, basil, salt and pepper. Carefully loosen the skin of each chicken breast on one side to form a pocket; stuff with vegetable mixture.

Coating Keepers

When making a coating or seasoning mix for your favorite chicken recipes, double or triple the amount. Then you can store the extra to use another day!

10 to 12 flour tortillas (6 inches)
Sour cream and additional salsa, optional

Place the first eight ingredients and 1/2 cup cheese in a food processor; blend until smooth. Spread evenly over tortillas. Roll up and place seam side down in a greased 13-in. x 9-in. x 2-in. baking dish. Cover and bake at 350° for 20 minutes or until heated through.

Sprinkle with remaining cheese; let stand until cheese melts. Serve with sour cream and salsa if desired. **Yield:** 10-12 servings.

Editor's Note: When cutting or seeding hot peppers, use rubber or plastic gloves to protect your hands. Avoid touching your face.

Bruschetta Chicken

(Pictured at right)

Carolin Cattoi-Demkiw, Lethbridge, Alberta

My husband and I enjoy serving this tasty chicken to company as well as family. It looks like we fussed, but it's really fast and easy to fix. I found the recipe years ago and have made this dish many times.

✓ Uses less fat, sugar or salt. Includes Nutritional Analysis and Diabetic Exchanges.

- 1/2 cup all-purpose flour
- 1/2 cup egg substitute
- 4 boneless skinless chicken breast halves (1 pound)
- 1/4 cup grated Parmesan cheese
- 1/4 cup dry bread crumbs
- 1 tablespoon butter, melted
- 2 large tomatoes, seeded and chopped
- 3 tablespoons minced fresh basil
- 2 garlic cloves, minced
- 1 tablespoon olive oil
- 1/2 teaspoon salt
- 1/4 teaspoon pepper

Place flour and eggs in separate shallow bowls. Dip chicken in flour, then in eggs; place in a greased 13-in. x 9-in. x 2-in. baking dish. Combine the Parmesan cheese, bread crumbs and butter; sprinkle over chicken. Loosely cover baking dish with foil. Bake at 375° for 20 minutes. Uncover; bake 5-10 minutes longer or until chicken juices run clear.

Meanwhile, in a bowl, combine the remaining ingredients. Spoon over the chicken. Return to the oven for 3-5 minutes or until tomato mixture is heated through. **Yield:** 4 servings.

Nutritional Analysis: One serving equals 358 calories, 13 g fat (5 g saturated fat), 86 mg cholesterol, 623 mg sodium, 22 g carbohydrate, 2 g fiber, 36 g protein. **Diabetic Exchanges:** 4-1/2 lean meat, 1 starch, 1 vegetable.

Curry Chicken

Tim Buckmaster, Millsboro, Delaware

I learned this recipe while in college. I used a large-scale version of this recipe to feed 20 hungry fellow students. Everyone complimented the tasty combination of tomato and spices.

- 1 cup dry bread crumbs
- 3/4 teaspoon salt
- 1/2 teaspoon paprika
- 1/4 teaspoon pepper
- 1/8 teaspoon ground ginger
- 1 broiler/fryer chicken (3 to 4 pounds), cut up
- 1/4 cup butter
- 1/2 cup chopped green pepper
- 1/4 cup chopped onion
- 1 garlic clove, minced
- 1 can (14-1/2 ounces) stewed tomatoes
- 1 to 1-1/2 teaspoons curry powder
- 1/2 teaspoon dried thyme
Hot cooked rice

In a shallow bowl, combine the bread crumbs, salt, paprika, pepper and ginger; coat chicken pieces. In a large skillet, brown chicken in butter. Transfer to a greased 13-in. x 9-in. x 2-in. baking dish and set aside.

In the same skillet, saute the green pepper, onion and garlic until tender. Stir in tomatoes, curry and thyme. Pour over chicken. Bake, uncovered, at 350° for 30-35 minutes or until juices run clear. Serve over rice. **Yield:** 4-6 servings.

Cover and bake at 350° for 30 minutes. Uncover and sprinkle with cheese; return to the oven for 15 minutes or until cheese is melted and bubbly. Garnish with parsley. **Yield:** 8 servings.

Sunday Fried Chicken

(Pictured below and on back cover)

Audrey Read, Fraser Lake, British Columbia

Like most fried chicken recipes, the chicken is coated and browned in oil. This recipe, however, adds the convenient step of finishing the cooking in the oven.

      2 cups all-purpose flour
  1/2 cup cornmeal
      2 tablespoons salt
      2 tablespoons ground mustard
      2 tablespoons paprika
      2 tablespoons garlic salt
      1 tablespoon celery salt
      1 tablespoon pepper
      1 teaspoon ground ginger
  1/2 teaspoon dried thyme
  1/2 teaspoon dried oregano
      1 broiler/fryer chicken (3 to 4 pounds), cut up
Vegetable oil

Combine the first 11 ingredients. Place about 1 cup flour mixture in a large resealable plastic bag. Add a few chicken pieces to the bag at a time; shake to coat.

Heat 1/4 in. of oil in large skillet on medium-high. Brown chicken on all sides; transfer to an ungreased 13-in. x 9-in. x 2-in. baking pan. Bake, uncovered, at 350°

Spinach Chicken Enchiladas

(Pictured above)

Joy Headley, Grand Prairie, Texas

This recipe is a favorite and a nice change from the usual beef enchiladas.

      4 boneless skinless chicken breast halves,
          cut into thin strips
  1/4 cup chopped onion
      1 package (10 ounces) frozen chopped
          spinach, thawed and well drained
      1 can (10-3/4 ounces) condensed cream of
          mushroom soup, undiluted
  3/4 cup milk
      1 cup (8 ounces) sour cream
      1 teaspoon ground nutmeg
      1 teaspoon garlic powder
      1 teaspoon onion powder
      2 cups (8 ounces) shredded mozzarella cheese
      8 flour tortillas (8 inches)
Minced fresh parsley

Coat a large skillet with nonstick cooking spray; cook and stir chicken and onion over medium heat for 6-8 minutes or until chicken is no longer pink. Remove from heat; add spinach and mix well.

In a bowl, combine soup, milk, sour cream and seasonings; mix well. Stir 3/4 cup into chicken and spinach mixture. Divide mixture evenly among tortillas.

Roll up and place, seam side down, in a 13-in. x 9-in. x 2-in. baking pan that has been sprayed with nonstick cooking spray. Pour the remaining soup mixture over enchiladas.

for 45-55 minutes or until juices run clear. Recipe makes enough coating for three chickens. Store unused mixture in an airtight container. **Yield:** 4-6 servings.

rolling boil; boil for 1 minute. Reduce heat; simmer, uncovered for 10-15 minutes or until thickened. Brush over wings.

Bake 20-25 minutes longer, turning and basting once, or until the chicken juices run clear. **Yield:** 10-12 servings.

Raspberry Glazed Wings

Sue Seymour, Valatie, New York

These fruity glazed wings are a staple at our house. They're a super finger food when entertaining and also make a tasty entree.

  3/4 **cup seedless raspberry jam**
  1/4 **cup cider vinegar**
  1/4 **cup soy sauce**
    3 **garlic cloves, minced**
    1 **teaspoon pepper**
  16 **whole chicken wings (about 3 pounds)**

In a saucepan, combine jam, vinegar, soy sauce, garlic and pepper. Bring to a boil; boil for 1 minute. Cut chicken wings into three sections; discard wing tips. Place wings in a large bowl; add raspberry mixture and toss to coat. Cover and refrigerate for 4 hours.

Line a 15-in. x 10-in. x 1-in. baking pan with foil and heavily grease the foil. Using a slotted spoon and reserving the marinade, place wings in pan. Bake at 375° for 30 minutes, turning once.

Meanwhile, in a saucepan, bring marinade to a

Honey Garlic Chicken

(Pictured above)

The mellow flavor of chicken pairs well with honey, orange juice and garlic. This tasty dish from our Test Kitchen is certain to become a favorite.

    4 **boneless skinless chicken breast halves**
    2 **tablespoons honey**
    2 **tablespoons orange *or* lemon juice**
    1 **tablespoon vegetable oil**
  1/2 **teaspoon salt**
Dash pepper
    1 **to 2 garlic cloves, minced**

Place chicken in a greased 13-in. x 9-in. x 2-in. baking pan. Combine the remaining ingredients; pour over chicken. Bake, uncovered, at 400° for 15 minutes. Broil 4 to 6 in. from the heat for 5-7 minutes or until juices run clear, brushing occasionally with sauce. **Yield:** 4 servings.

7 Casseroles

Chicken Lasagna

(Pictured at left)

Dena Stapelman, Laurel, Nebraska

For a cooking class several years ago, I lightened up a classic lasagna and created this chicken version. It was preferred over the traditional dish in taste-tests in my class and by my family and friends as well.

✓ Uses less fat, sugar or salt. Includes Nutritional Analysis and Diabetic Exchanges.

  10 uncooked lasagna noodles
    1 pound boneless skinless chicken breasts
    1 can (14-1/2 ounces) diced tomatoes, undrained
    1 can (12 ounces) tomato paste
1-1/2 cups sliced fresh mushrooms
  1/4 cup chopped onion
    1 tablespoon dried basil
1-3/4 teaspoons salt, *divided*
  1/8 teaspoon garlic powder
    3 cups 2% small-curd cottage cheese
  1/2 cup egg substitute
  1/2 cup grated Parmesan cheese
  1/3 cup minced fresh parsley
  1/2 teaspoon pepper
    2 cups (8 ounces) shredded part-skim mozzarella cheese

Cook noodles according to package directions. Meanwhile, broil chicken 6 in. from the heat for 6-8 minutes on each side or until juices run clear; let stand for 15 minutes or until cool enough to handle. Shred chicken with two forks. Drain noodles; set aside.

In a large nonstick skillet, combine the shredded chicken, tomatoes, tomato paste, mushrooms, onion, basil, 3/4 teaspoon salt and garlic powder. Bring mixture to a boil. Reduce the heat; cover and simmer for 25-30 minutes.

In a bowl, combine the cottage cheese, egg substitute, grated Parmesan cheese, parsley, pepper and remaining salt.

In a 13-in. x 9-in. x 2-in. baking dish coated with nonstick cooking spray, place half of the noodles, overlapping them. Layer with half of the cheese mixture, half of the chicken mixture and half of the mozzarella. Repeat layers.

Cover and bake at 375° for 25-30 minutes or until bubbly. Uncover; bake 5 minutes longer. Let lasagna stand for 15 minutes before cutting. **Yield:** 12 servings.

Nutritional Analysis: One piece equals 240 calories, 7 g fat (4 g saturated fat), 43 mg cholesterol, 1,038 mg sodium, 17 g carbohydrate, 2 g fiber, 28 g protein. **Diabetic Exchanges:** 2 lean meat, 1 starch, 1 fat.

Mexican Chicken Manicotti

Keely Jankunas, Corvallis, Montana

This Italian specialty has a little Mexican zip. Be careful not to overcook the manicotti. If the filled shells happen to break, you can simply place them in the pan seam-side down.

    1 package (8 ounces) manicotti shells
    2 cups cubed cooked chicken
    2 cups (8 ounces) shredded Monterey Jack cheese, *divided*
1-1/2 cups (6 ounces) shredded cheddar cheese
    1 cup (8 ounces) sour cream
    1 small onion, diced, *divided*
    1 can (4 ounces) chopped green chilies, *divided*
    1 can (10-3/4 ounces) condensed cream of chicken soup, undiluted
    1 cup salsa
  2/3 cup milk

Cook the manicotti shells according to package directions. Meanwhile, in a large bowl, combine the chicken, 1-1/2 cups of the Monterey Jack cheese, cheddar cheese, sour cream, half of the onion and 6 tablespoons chilies.

In another bowl, combine the soup, salsa, milk, and remaining onion and chilies. Spread 1/2 cup in a greased 13-in. x 9-in. x 2-in. baking dish. Drain manicotti; stuff each with about 1/4 cup chicken mixture. Arrange over sauce in baking dish. Pour remaining sauce over shells.

Cover and bake at 350° for 30 minutes. Uncover; sprinkle with remaining Monterey Jack cheese. Bake 10 minutes longer or until cheese is melted. **Yield:** 7 servings.

Rotini Chicken Casserole

(Pictured at right)

Ruth Lee, Troy, Ontario

Pasta dishes are a favorite in our family. I changed the original recipe to suit our tastes…and we all think this comforting casserole is delicious. I like to accompany it with a tossed green salad.

 Uses less fat, sugar or salt. Includes Nutritional Analysis and Diabetic Exchanges.

2-3/4 cups uncooked tricolor rotini *or* spiral pasta
  3/4 cup chopped onion
  1/2 cup chopped celery
    2 garlic cloves, minced
    1 tablespoon canola oil
    3 cups cubed cooked chicken breast
    1 can (10-3/4 ounces) reduced-fat reduced-sodium condensed cream of chicken soup, undiluted
1-1/2 cups fat-free milk
    1 package (16 ounces) frozen Italian-blend vegetables
    1 cup (4 ounces) shredded reduced-fat cheddar cheese
    2 tablespoons minced fresh parsley
1-1/4 teaspoons dried thyme
    1 teaspoon salt
  2/3 cup crushed cornflakes

Cook pasta according to package directions. Meanwhile, in a nonstick skillet, saute onion, celery and garlic in oil until tender. Drain pasta; place in a bowl. Add the onion mixture, chicken, soup, milk, frozen vegetables, cheese, parsley, thyme and salt.

Pour into a shallow 3-qt. baking dish coated with nonstick cooking spray. Cover and bake at 350° for 25 minutes. Sprinkle with cornflakes; spritz with nonstick cooking spray. Bake, uncovered, 10-15 minutes longer or until heated through. **Yield:** 8 servings.

Nutritional Analysis: One serving (1-1/3 cups) equals 341 calories, 7 g fat (3 g saturated fat), 56 mg cholesterol, 698 mg sodium, 40 g carbohydrate, 3 g fiber, 28 g protein. **Diabetic Exchanges:** 3 lean meat, 2 starch, 1 vegetable.

Chicken Wild Rice Dish

(Pictured at left)

This handy recipe from our Test Kitchen staff serves up enough for a potluck or reunion. The blend of veggies, rice and chicken is wonderful.

    2 pounds sliced fresh mushrooms
    4 cups chopped celery
    4 cups chopped sweet red pepper
2-2/3 cups chopped green onions
    8 garlic cloves, minced
1-1/3 cups butter
    4 cans (14-1/2 ounces *each*) chicken broth
  24 cups cubed cooked chicken
  16 cups cooked wild rice
  16 cups cooked long grain rice

Select poultry well within the "sell by" date shown on the packaging. The packages should be well-sealed and free of tears. Make sure that the frozen poultry you purchase is solidly frozen.

The amount of poultry you need varies with the type and cut:
- Boneless chicken cuts yield 3 to 4 servings per pound.
- Whole and bone-in chicken parts yield 1 to 2 servings per pound.

- 8 cups (2 pounds) shredded cheddar cheese
- 3 tablespoons salt
- 3 tablespoons dried basil
- 2 teaspoons pepper

In a kettle, saute the first five ingredients in butter until tender. Add remaining ingredients and mix well. Spoon into four greased 13-in. x 9-in. x 2-in. baking dishes.

Cover and bake at 350° for 75 minutes. Uncover and bake 15 minutes longer or until heated through. **Yield:** 50 servings.

Chicken Rice Casserole

(Pictured at right)

Marcia Hostetter, Canton, New York

This dish can be doubly thrifty because of the Homemade Seasoned Rice Mix. After using the cup of it the casserole calls for for this meal, you can use the remainder of the rice mix as a gift or as a side dish with meat another day.

- 2-1/2 cups cubed cooked chicken
- 1-1/2 cups frozen mixed vegetables
- 1 cup Homemade Seasoned Rice Mix (recipe above right)
- 1/2 cup chopped onion
- 1 can (4 ounces) mushroom stems and pieces, drained
- 2 cups water
- 1 can (10-3/4 ounces) condensed cream of chicken soup, undiluted
- 1/4 teaspoon onion salt
- 1/4 teaspoon dried thyme
- 1/4 cup crushed potato chips

In a greased 2-qt. casserole, combine chicken, vegetables, rice mix, onion and mushrooms. Combine water, soup, onion salt and thyme; mix well. Pour over the rice mixture; stir.

Cover and bake at 375° for 55-65 minutes or until the rice is tender, stirring occasionally. Sprinkle with potato chips. **Yield:** 6 servings.

Homemade Seasoned Rice Mix

Marcia Hostetter, Canton, New York

- 3 cups uncooked long grain rice
- 6 teaspoons instant chicken bouillon granules
- 1/4 cup dried parsley flakes
- 2 teaspoons onion powder
- 1/2 teaspoon garlic powder
- 1/4 teaspoon dried thyme

Combine all ingredients in a storage container with a tight-fitting lid. **Yield:** 3-1/2 cups.

Editor's Note: To prepare rice as a side dish, combine 2 cups water and 1 tablespoon butter in a saucepan; bring to a boil. Stir in 1 cup mix. Reduce heat; cover and simmer for 15-20 minutes. **Yield:** 6 servings.

Corn Bread Chicken Bake

Madge Britton, Afton, Tennessee

To make the most of leftover corn bread, try this hearty main-dish casserole. It's moist, delicious and good on any occasion.

1-1/4 pounds boneless skinless chicken breasts
    6 cups cubed corn bread
    8 bread slices, cubed
    1 medium onion, chopped
    2 cans (10-3/4 ounces *each*) condensed cream of chicken soup, undiluted
    1 cup chicken broth
    2 tablespoons butter, melted
1-1/2 to 2 teaspoons rubbed sage
    1 teaspoon salt
  1/2 to 1 teaspoon pepper

Place chicken in a large skillet and cover with water; bring to a boil. Reduce heat; cover and simmer for 12-14 minutes or until juices run clear. Drain and cut into cubes.

In a large bowl, combine the corn bread, cubed bread, onion, soup, broth, butter, sage, salt and pepper. Add chicken. Transfer to a greased 13-in. x 9-in. x 2-in. baking dish. Bake casserole, uncovered, at 350° for 45 minutes or until heated through. **Yield:** 8-10 servings.

Chicken in Every Pot Pie

(Pictured above)

Mary Beth de Ribeaux, Gaithersburg, Maryland

I created a new title for my mom's potpie recipe while trying to come up with a clever menu for our Presidents' Day party. An old political slogan came to mind that fit the theme and my main dish just fine! It's chock-full of chicken and vegetables.

    4 cups cubed cooked chicken
1-1/2 cups chicken broth
1-1/2 cups frozen peas
    3 to 4 medium carrots, cut into 1/4-inch slices
    1 can (10-3/4 ounces) condensed cream of mushroom soup, undiluted
  1/4 teaspoon salt
  1/4 teaspoon pepper
    2 cups biscuit/baking mix
1-1/4 cups milk
    1 teaspoon garlic powder
  1/2 teaspoon celery seed
Paprika

In a saucepan, combine the cooked chicken, broth, peas, carrots, soup, salt and pepper; bring to a boil, stirring occasionally.

Meanwhile, combine the biscuit mix, milk, garlic powder and celery seed in a mixing bowl (mixture will be thin).

Pour the hot chicken mixture into eight greased ovenproof 10-oz. custard cups or casseroles. Immediately spoon 1/4 cup of the biscuit mixture evenly on top of each custard cup. Sprinkle with paprika.

Bake, uncovered, at 350° for 30-35 minutes or until the topping is golden brown and filling is bubbly. **Yield:** 8 servings.

Chicken Celery Casserole

Ruth Andrewson, Peck, Idaho

When time is short and I have many guests, this is the recipe I reach for. The comforting dish has a crunchy topping and can be on the table in under an hour.

    4 cups cubed cooked chicken
    8 celery ribs, thinly sliced
    1 cup chopped pecans
    1 small onion, diced
    2 cups mayonnaise
    1 tablespoon lemon juice
    1 teaspoon garlic salt
    1 cup crushed potato chips
    1 cup crushed french-fried onions
  1/2 cup shredded cheddar cheese

In a bowl, combine chicken, celery, pecans and diced onion. Combine mayonnaise, lemon juice and garlic salt; add to chicken mixture and mix well. Transfer to a greased 13-in. x 9-in. x 2-in. baking dish.

Bake, uncovered, at 350° for 20 minutes. Top with potato chips, french-fried onions and cheese. Bake 5-10 minutes longer or until chips are crisp and cheese is melted. **Yield:** 8 servings.

Editor's Note: Reduced-fat or fat-free mayonnaise may not be substituted for regular mayonnaise in this recipe.

Chicken 'n' Biscuits

(Pictured below)

Marilyn Minnick, Hillsboro, Indiana

This comforting casserole has a colorful medley of vegetables and chunky chicken that's topped with golden homemade biscuits.

✓ Uses less fat, sugar or salt. Includes Nutritional Analysis and Diabetic Exchanges.

- 1 medium onion, chopped
- 2 teaspoons vegetable oil
- 1/4 cup all-purpose flour
- 1/2 teaspoon dried basil
- 1/2 teaspoon dried thyme
- 1/4 teaspoon pepper
- 2-1/2 cups fat-free milk
- 1 tablespoon Worcestershire sauce
- 1 package (16 ounces) frozen mixed vegetables
- 2 cups cubed cooked chicken
- 2 tablespoons grated Parmesan cheese

BISCUITS:
- 1 cup all-purpose flour
- 1 tablespoon sugar
- 1-1/2 teaspoons baking powder
- 1/4 teaspoon salt
- 1/3 cup skim milk
- 3 tablespoons vegetable oil
- 1 tablespoon minced fresh parsley

In a saucepan, saute onion in oil until tender. Stir in the flour, basil, thyme and pepper until blended. Gradually stir in milk and Worcestershire sauce until smooth. Bring to a boil; boil and stir for 2 minutes. Stir in the vegetables, chicken and Parmesan cheese; reduce the heat to low.

Meanwhile, combine flour, sugar, baking powder and salt in a bowl. Combine milk, oil and parsley; stir into dry ingredients just until combined. Transfer hot chicken mixture to a greased 2-1/2-qt. baking dish.

Drop biscuit batter by rounded tablespoonfuls onto chicken mixture. Bake, uncovered, at 375° for 30-40 minutes or until biscuits are lightly browned. **Yield:** 8 servings.

Nutritional Analysis: One serving equals 246 calories, 284 mg sodium, 24 mg cholesterol, 31 g carbohydrate, 13 g protein, 8 g fat. **Diabetic Exchanges:** 2 starch, 1 meat, 1/2 fat.

french-fried onions; bake 5 minutes longer. **Yield:** 2 casseroles (4-6 servings each).

Chicken Chili Tortilla Bake

(Pictured below)

Cindee Rolston, St. Marys, West Virginia

This saucy lasagna is my adaptation of a chicken enchilada recipe. The dish has become very popular with my co-workers after I shared leftovers one day for lunch.

   2 packages (3 ounces *each*) cream cheese, softened
   1 medium onion, chopped
   8 green onions, chopped
   2 cups (8 ounces) shredded Mexican-cheese blend, *divided*
   2 garlic cloves, minced
3/4 teaspoon ground cumin, *divided*
1/2 teaspoon minced fresh cilantro
   3 cups cubed cooked chicken
1/4 cup butter
1/4 cup all-purpose flour
1-1/2 cups chicken broth
   1 cup (4 ounces) shredded Monterey Jack cheese
   1 cup (8 ounces) sour cream

Green Bean Chicken Casserole

(Pictured above)

DeLissa Mingee, Warr Acres, Oklahoma

My husband asked for seconds the first time I made this. It's starts with cooked chicken and frozen green beans.

   1 package (6 ounces) long grain and wild rice mix
   4 cups cubed cooked chicken
1-3/4 cups frozen French-style green beans
   1 can (10-3/4 ounces) condensed cream of mushroom soup, undiluted
   1 can (10-3/4 ounces) condensed cream of chicken and broccoli soup, undiluted
   1 can (4 ounces) mushroom stems and pieces, drained
2/3 cup chopped onion
2/3 cup chopped green pepper
   1 envelope onion soup mix
3/4 cup shredded Colby cheese
ADDITIONAL INGREDIENT (for each casserole):
   2/3 cup french-fried onions

Prepare wild rice according to package directions. Stir in chicken, beans, soups, mushrooms, onion, green pepper and soup mix. Spoon into two greased 1-1/2-qt. baking dishes. Sprinkle with cheese. Cover and freeze one casserole for up to 3 months.

Cover and bake the second casserole at 350° for 25-30 minutes or until heated through. Uncover and sprinkle with french-fried onions; bake 5 minutes longer or until onions are golden.

To use frozen casserole: Completely thaw in the refrigerator. Remove from the refrigerator 30 minutes before baking. Cover and bake at 350° for 60-65 minutes or until heated through. Uncover and sprinkle with

1 can (4 ounces) chopped green chilies, drained
1/8 teaspoon dried thyme
1/8 teaspoon salt
1/8 teaspoon pepper
12 flour tortillas (6 inches), halved

In a mixing bowl, combine cream cheese, onions, 1-1/2 cups Mexican-cheese blend, garlic, 1/4 teaspoon cumin and cilantro. Stir in chicken; set aside.

In a saucepan, melt butter. Stir in flour until smooth; gradually add broth. Bring to a boil; cook and stir for 2 minutes or until thickened. Remove from the heat.

Stir in Monterey Jack cheese, sour cream, chilies, thyme, salt, pepper and remaining cumin. Spread 1/2 cup of the cheese sauce in a greased 13-in. x 9-in. x 2-in. baking dish.

Top with six tortilla halves, a third of the chicken mixture and a fourth of the cheese sauce. Repeat tortilla, chicken and cheese sauce layers twice. Top with remaining tortillas, cheese sauce and Mexican cheese.

Cover and bake at 350° for 30 minutes. Uncover and bake 10 minutes longer or until heated through. Let stand 5 minutes before cutting. **Yield:** 12 servings.

Artichoke Chicken Lasagna

Donna Boellner, Annapolis, Maryland

Chicken, artichokes and a cream sauce make this lasagna more special than the usual tomato and beef variety.

2/3 cup butter, *divided*
1/3 cup all-purpose flour
1 teaspoon salt, *divided*
1/4 teaspoon ground nutmeg
1/8 teaspoon pepper
3 cups milk
1-3/4 pounds boneless skinless chicken breasts, cut into thin strips and halved
2 cans (14 ounces *each*) water-packed artichoke hearts, drained and quartered
1 teaspoon dried thyme
9 lasagna noodles, cooked and drained
1 cup grated Parmesan cheese

In a saucepan, melt 1/3 cup butter. Stir in flour, 1/2 teaspoon salt, nutmeg and pepper until smooth. Gradually stir in milk. Bring to a boil; cook and stir for 2 minutes or until thickened. In a skillet, cook chicken in remaining butter until juices run clear. Stir in artichokes, thyme and remaining salt; heat through.

In a greased 13-in. x 9-in. x 2-in. baking dish, layer about 1/3 cup white sauce, three noodles, 1/2 cup sauce, 1/3 cup Parmesan cheese and about 3 cups chicken mixture. Repeat layers. Top with remaining noodles, sauce and Parmesan cheese. Bake, uncovered, at 350° for 35-40 minutes or until bubbly. Let stand for 10 minutes before cutting. **Yield:** 12 servings.

Chicken and Asparagus

(Pictured above)

Ramona Ruskell, Columbia, Missouri

You can greet guests with a taste of springtime when this chicken and asparagus casserole is on the menu. It bakes in just half an hour. People savor the rich cheesy sauce, and it freezes well, too.

1 medium onion, chopped
1/4 cup butter
1 can (10-3/4 ounces) condensed cream of mushroom soup, undiluted
1 can (8 ounces) mushroom stems and pieces, drained
1 can (5 ounces) evaporated milk
2 tablespoons chopped pimientos
2 teaspoons soy sauce
1/2 teaspoon pepper
1/4 teaspoon hot pepper sauce
2 cups (8 ounces) shredded cheddar cheese
5 to 5-1/2 cups cubed cooked chicken
1 package (10 ounces) frozen cut asparagus, thawed
3 tablespoons chopped almonds

In a large saucepan, saute onion in butter until tender. Stir in the soup, mushrooms, milk, pimientos, soy sauce, pepper and pepper sauce. Stir in cheese until melted.

In a greased shallow 2-1/2-qt. baking dish, layer half of the chicken, asparagus and cheese sauce. Repeat the layers. Sprinkle with almonds. Bake, uncovered, at 350° for 25-30 minutes or until bubbly. **Yield:** 8-10 servings.

8 Turkey Prize-Winners

Herb-Roasted Turkey

(Pictured at left)

Becky Goldsmith, Eden Prairie, Minnesota

Our guests always comment on how moist and flavorful this elegant entree is. Rubbed with garden-fresh herbs, this turkey has such a wonderful aroma when it's roasting that it lures everyone into the kitchen!

- 1 turkey (14 pounds)
- 1 tablespoon salt
- 1 teaspoon pepper
- 18 sprigs fresh thyme, *divided*
- 4 medium onions, sliced
- 4 celery ribs, sliced
- 2 medium carrots, sliced
- 3 bay leaves
- 1 tablespoon peppercorns
- 1/2 cup butter, melted
- 1 teaspoon minced fresh sage *or* 1/2 teaspoon rubbed sage
- 1 teaspoon minced fresh thyme *or* 1/2 teaspoon dried thyme
- 1 teaspoon minced chives

Rub the surface of the turkey and sprinkle cavity with salt and pepper. Place the 12 sprigs of thyme in the turkey cavity.

In a large heavy roasting pan, place the onions, celery, carrots, bay leaves, peppercorns and remaining thyme sprigs.

Place the turkey, breast side up, over vegetables. Drizzle butter over turkey and sprinkle with minced herbs. Cover loosely with foil.

Preparing Turkey for Roasting

- It is recommended to thaw frozen poultry in the refrigerator. Plan on 24 hours for every 5 pounds. For example, a 20-pound turkey will need to thaw in the refrigerator for 4 days.
- Make sure whole birds are completely thawed before stuffing and/or roasting, or the roasting times will need to be increased and internal temperature checked often.

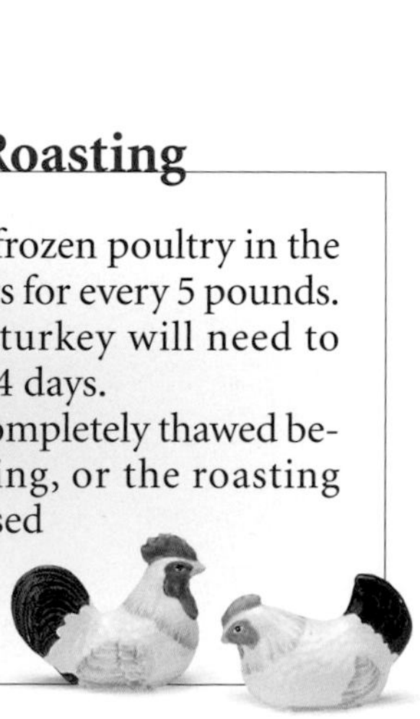

Bake at 325° for 2-1/2 hours. Remove foil; bake 1-1/2 to 2 hours longer or until a meat thermometer reads 180°, basting every 20 minutes. Cover and let stand for 20 minutes before carving. Discard bay leaves and peppercorns; thicken pan drippings for gravy if desired. **Yield:** 12-14 servings.

Saucy Turkey Meatballs

Janell Fugitt, Cimarron, Kansas

It's easy to turn lean ground turkey into these moist, tender meatballs. Ideal for informal gatherings of family and friends, the appetizers feature a tangy sauce that my guests find delicious.

✓ Uses less fat, sugar or salt. Includes Nutritional Analysis and Diabetic Exchanges.

- 1 cup old-fashioned oats
- 3/4 cup fat-free evaporated milk
- 1 medium onion, chopped
- 1 teaspoon salt
- 1 teaspoon chili powder
- 1/4 teaspoon garlic salt
- 1/4 teaspoon pepper
- 1-1/2 pounds lean ground turkey
- SAUCE:
- 2 cups ketchup
- 1-1/2 cups packed brown sugar
- 1/4 cup chopped onion
- 2 tablespoons Liquid Smoke, optional
- 1/2 teaspoon garlic salt

In a bowl, combine the oats, milk, onion, salt, chili powder, garlic salt and pepper. Crumble turkey over mixture and mix well.

Shape into 1-in. balls. Place in a 13-in. x 9-in. x 2-in. baking dish coated with nonstick cooking spray. Bake, uncovered, at 350° for 10-15 minutes.

Combine the sauce ingredients; pour over meatballs. Bake 30-35 minutes longer or until meat is no longer pink. **Yield:** 15 servings.

Nutritional Analysis: One serving (3 meatballs) equals 217 calories, 4 g fat (1 g saturated fat), 36 mg cholesterol, 695 mg sodium, 36 g carbohydrate, 1 g fiber, 10 g protein. **Diabetic Exchanges:** 2 starch, 1 lean meat.

1/3 cup butter
1/2 cup ketchup
1/4 cup packed brown sugar
3 tablespoons Worcestershire sauce
1-1/2 teaspoons chili powder
1 teaspoon salt
1/8 teaspoon pepper
1/8 teaspoon hot pepper sauce
4 cups shredded cooked turkey
8 hamburger buns, split, toasted and buttered

In a saucepan, saute the celery, onion and green pepper in butter until tender. Add the next seven ingredients. Bring to a boil. Reduce heat; cover and simmer for 5 minutes. Add turkey; heat through. Serve on buns. **Yield:** 8 servings.

Turkey Potato Pancakes

Kathi Duerr, Fulda, Minnesota

(Pictured above)

My husband likes pancakes, and I appreciate quick suppers...so I gave this recipe a try when I saw it. The addition of turkey turns golden side-dish potato pancakes into a simple main dish we all savor.

3 eggs
3 cups shredded peeled potatoes
1-1/2 cups finely chopped cooked turkey
1/4 cup sliced green onions with tops
2 tablespoons all-purpose flour
1-1/2 teaspoons salt
Vegetable oil
Cranberry sauce, optional

In a bowl, beat the eggs. Add potatoes, turkey, onions, flour and salt; mix well. Heat about 1/4 in. of oil in a large skillet. Pour batter by 1/3 cupfuls into hot oil. Fry 5-6 minutes on each side or until potatoes are tender and pancakes are golden brown. Serve with cranberry sauce if desired. **Yield:** 12 pancakes.

Barbecued Turkey Sandwiches

Pamela Siegrist, Fort Recovery, Ohio

I have an excellent source for turkey recipes, since many of our neighbors are poultry farmers! These tasty sandwiches are a great way to use up leftover holiday turkey.

2 celery ribs, chopped
1/2 cup chopped onion
1/4 cup chopped green pepper

Turkey Primavera

(Pictured below)

Zita Wilensky, N. Miami Beach, Florida

We grow herbs and vegetables in our garden, so I incorporate them into recipes whenever possible. This creation has tender turkey and mushrooms, onions and green pepper covered in a zippy tomato sauce.

1/4 cup all-purpose flour
2 teaspoons minced fresh parsley
1-1/2 pounds turkey tenderloins, cubed
2 tablespoons olive oil
1/2 cup chicken broth
1 cup sliced fresh mushrooms
1 medium onion, chopped

4 garlic cloves, minced
1/2 medium green pepper, chopped
1 can (14-1/2 ounces) beef broth
3/4 cup tomato puree
1/2 teaspoon dried thyme
1/2 teaspoon dried rosemary, crushed
1/2 teaspoon dried basil
1 bay leaf
1/4 teaspoon salt
1/8 teaspoon pepper
Hot cooked fettuccine *or* spaghetti
Parmesan cheese, optional

Combine flour and parsley; add turkey and toss to coat. In a skillet, brown turkey in oil; remove with a slotted spoon and set aside. In the same skillet, combine chicken broth, mushrooms, onion, garlic and green pepper. Cook and stir for 3-4 minutes. Add beef broth, tomato puree and seasonings.

Cook and stir for 20-25 minutes or until sauce is desired consistency. Add turkey; heat through. Remove the bay leaf. Serve over pasta; sprinkle with Parmesan if desired. **Yield:** 4-6 servings.

Creamy Turkey Soup

(Pictured above right)

Kathleen Harris, Galesburg, Illinois

My mother always prepared a holiday turkey much larger than our family could ever eat in one meal so there'd be plenty of leftovers. That's one tradition I've kept up. This hearty soup uses a lot of turkey and is great after watching football games and raking leaves.

1 large onion, chopped
3 celery ribs with leaves, cut into 1/4-inch pieces
6 tablespoons butter
6 tablespoons all-purpose flour
1 teaspoon salt
1/4 teaspoon pepper
1/4 teaspoon garlic powder
1/2 teaspoon *each* dried thyme, savory and parsley flakes
1-1/2 cups milk
4 cups cubed cooked turkey
5 medium carrots, cut into 1/4-inch pieces
1 to 2 cups turkey *or* chicken broth
1 package (10 ounces) frozen peas

In a large kettle, saute onion and celery in butter until tender, about 10 minutes. Stir in the flour and seasonings; gradually add milk, stirring constantly until thickened. Add turkey and carrots. Add enough broth until soup is desired consistency.

Cover and simmer for 15 minutes. Add peas; cover and simmer for 15 minutes or until vegetables are tender. **Yield:** 6-8 servings (2 quarts).

Turkey Drumstick Dinner

Alice Balliet, Kane, Pennsylvania

I discovered this recipe a long time ago and love it since it uses tasty economical turkey drumsticks. Our family and friends enjoy this savory meat and potatoes meal.

4 uncooked turkey drumsticks (about 3 pounds)
2 tablespoons vegetable oil
1 tablespoon butter
1 medium onion, sliced
1 can (14-1/2 ounces) stewed tomatoes
3 chicken bouillon cubes
1 teaspoon garlic salt
1/2 teaspoon dried oregano
1/2 teaspoon dried basil
4 large potatoes, peeled, cooked and quartered
2 medium zucchini, cut into 3/4-inch slices
2 tablespoons cornstarch
2 tablespoons water
Chopped fresh parsley

In a large skillet, brown drumsticks in oil and butter. Place in a 3-qt. Dutch oven. Top with onion slices. In the same skillet, heat tomatoes, bouillon and seasonings until bouillon is dissolved. Pour over the drumsticks.

Cover and bake at 325° for 2 hours, basting once or twice. Add potatoes and zucchini. Cover and bake for 20 minutes. Remove drumsticks and vegetables to a serving dish and keep warm. Combine cornstarch and water until smooth; stir into tomato mixture. Return to the oven, uncovered, for 10-15 minutes or until slightly thickened. Pour over drumsticks and vegetables. Sprinkle with parsley. **Yield:** 4 servings.

Apple-Almond Stuffed Turkey

(Pictured above)

Laurel McLennan, Medicine Hat, Alberta

I tried this terrific recipe out on some friends at a party. Everyone enjoyed the combination of flavors and unique ingredients. It has become my "staple." The currants and apples give the stuffing a nice sweet flavor.

      1 loaf (1 pound) sliced bread
      3 medium onions, chopped
      3 medium tart apples, chopped
  1-1/2 cups diced fully cooked ham
      1 cup sliced celery
      1 tablespoon dried savory
      2 teaspoons grated lemon peel
  1-1/2 teaspoons grated orange peel
      1 teaspoon salt
    1/2 teaspoon pepper
    1/2 teaspoon fennel seed, crushed
    1/2 cup butter
  1-1/2 cups slivered almonds, toasted
    1/2 cup dried currants
      1 cup turkey *or* chicken broth
    1/2 cup apple juice
      1 turkey (14 to 16 pounds)

Cut bread into 1/2-in. cubes and place in a single layer on ungreased baking sheets. Bake at 225° for 30-40 minutes, tossing occasionally until partially dried. Meanwhile, in a skillet, saute next 10 ingredients in butter until onions and apple are tender, about 15 minutes.

Transfer to a large bowl. Add the bread cubes, almonds, currants, broth and juice; toss well. Just before baking, stuff the turkey. Skewer openings; tie drumsticks together. Place on a rack in a roasting pan. Bake, uncovered, at 325° for 4-1/2 to 5 hours or until thermometer reads 185° for turkey and 165° for stuffing. When turkey begins to brown, cover lightly with foil and baste if needed. **Yield:** 12 servings (12 cups stuffing).

Editor's Note: Stuffing may be baked separately in a greased 3-qt. baking dish. Cover and bake at 325° for 1 hour; uncover and bake 10 minutes.

Turkey in a Hurry

Denise Goedeken, Platte Center, Nebraska

This dish is easy to prepare and really brings some variety to mealtime. It's a delicious non-traditional way to fix turkey, which cooks up moist and tasty.

      2 turkey tenderloins (1-1/2 pounds)
    1/4 cup butter
    3/4 teaspoon dried thyme
    1/2 teaspoon dried rosemary, crushed
    1/4 teaspoon paprika
    1/8 teaspoon garlic powder

Cut tenderloins in half lengthwise, then into serving-size pieces. Place on rack of broiler pan. In a small saucepan, heat remaining ingredients until butter is melted.

Broil turkey until lightly browned on one side. Brush with herb butter; turn and brown other side. Brush with butter. Continue cooking 6-8 minutes or until no longer pink, brushing often with butter. **Yield:** 6 servings.

Turkey Lime Kabobs

(Pictured at right)

Shelly Johnston, Rochester, Minnesota

My husband loves to grill these deliciously different turkey kabobs, and everyone gets a kick out of the zingy taste from the limes and jalapenos. Its tongue-tingling combination of flavors always draws compliments.

      3 cans (6 ounces each) orange juice concentrate, thawed
  1-1/4 cups lime juice
      1 cup honey
      4 to 5 jalapeno peppers, seeded and chopped
     10 garlic cloves, minced
      3 tablespoons ground cumin
      2 tablespoons grated lime peel
      1 teaspoon salt
      2 pounds boneless turkey, chicken *or* pork, cut into 1-1/4-inch cubes
      4 medium sweet red *or* green peppers, cut into 1-inch pieces
      1 large red onion, cut into 1-inch pieces
      3 small zucchini, cut into 3/4-inch slices
      8 ounces fresh mushrooms
      3 medium limes, cut into wedges

In a bowl, combine the first eight ingredients; mix well. Pour half of marinade into a large resealable plastic bag; add meat and turn to coat. Pour remaining marinade into another large resealable plastic bag. Add vegetables and turn to coat. Seal and refrigerate for 8 hours or overnight, turning occasionally.

Drain meat, discarding marinade. Drain vegetables, reserving marinade for basting. On metal or soaked bamboo skewers, alternate meat, vegetables and lime wedges. Grill, uncovered, over medium heat for 4-5 minutes on each side. Baste with reserved marinade. Continue turning and basting for 10-12 minutes or until the meat juices run clear and vegetables are tender. **Yield:** 8 servings.

Editor's Note: When cutting or seeding hot peppers, use rubber or plastic gloves to protect your hands. Avoid touching your face.

Turkey Pasta Supreme

(Pictured at left)

Cassie Dion, S. Burlington, Vermont

Since this dish combines turkey and pasta, even our children love it. It's fun to make turkey a different way, and you can't beat the creamy, cheesy sauce.

    3/4 pound uncooked turkey breast
      2 garlic cloves, minced
      2 tablespoons butter
  1-1/4 cups heavy whipping cream
      2 tablespoons minced fresh basil *or* 2 teaspoons dried basil
    1/4 cup grated Parmesan cheese
         Dash pepper
      3 to 4 cups hot cooked pasta

Cut turkey into 2-in. x 1/4-in. pieces. In a skillet, saute turkey and garlic in butter until turkey is browned and no longer pink, about 6 minutes. Add cream, basil, Parmesan and pepper; bring to a boil.

Reduce heat; simmer for 3 minutes, stirring frequently. Stir in pasta and toss to coat. Serve immediately. **Yield:** 4 servings.

Turkey Biscuit Potpie

(Pictured below)

Shirley Francey, St. Catharines, Ontario

My family enjoys this comforting dish that is loaded with chunks of turkey, potatoes, carrots and green beans. Topped with easy-to-make biscuits, it has wonderful down-home flavor.

    1 large onion, chopped
    1 garlic clove, minced
1-1/2 cups cubed peeled potatoes
1-1/2 cups sliced carrots
    1 cup frozen cut green beans, thawed
    1 cup chicken broth
4-1/2 teaspoons all-purpose flour
    1 can (10-3/4 ounces) condensed cream of
      mushroom soup, undiluted
    2 cups cubed cooked turkey
    2 tablespoons minced fresh parsley
  1/2 teaspoon dried basil
  1/2 teaspoon dried thyme
  1/4 teaspoon pepper
BISCUITS:
    1 cup all-purpose flour
    2 teaspoons baking powder
  1/2 teaspoon dried oregano
    2 tablespoons cold butter
    7 tablespoons milk

In a large saucepan coated with nonstick cooking spray, cook onion and garlic over medium heat until tender. Add the potatoes, carrots, beans and broth; bring to a boil. Reduce heat; cover and simmer for 15-20 minutes or until potatoes are tender. Remove from the heat.

Combine the flour and mushroom soup; stir into vegetable mixture. Add the turkey and seasonings. Transfer to a 2-qt. baking dish coated with nonstick cooking spray.

In a bowl, combine the flour, baking powder and oregano. Cut in butter until evenly distributed. Stir in milk. Drop batter in six mounds onto the hot turkey mixture.

Bake, uncovered, at 400° for 20-25 minutes or until a toothpick inserted in the center of biscuits comes out clean and the biscuits are golden brown. **Yield:** 6 servings.

Peppery Herbed Turkey Tenderloin

(Pictured above)

Virginia Anthony, Blowing Rock, North Carolina

I won the North Carolina Turkey Cook-Off one year with these full-flavored tenderloins and rich sauce. Marinating the turkey in wine, garlic, rosemary and thyme gives it a fantastic taste.

    3 turkey tenderloins (12 ounces *each*)
    1 cup dry white wine *or* 1 cup apple juice
    3 green onions, chopped
    3 tablespoons minced fresh parsley
    6 teaspoons olive oil, *divided*
    1 tablespoon finely chopped garlic
  3/4 teaspoon dried rosemary, crushed
  3/4 teaspoon dried thyme
    1 teaspoon coarsely ground pepper

3/4 teaspoon salt, *divided*
4 teaspoons cornstarch
1 cup chicken broth

Pat tenderloins dry; flatten to 3/4-in. thickness. In a bowl, combine the wine or juice, onions, parsley, 4 teaspoons oil, garlic, rosemary and thyme; mix well. Pour 3/4 cup marinade into a large resealable plastic bag; add turkey. Seal and turn to coat; refrigerate for at least 4 hours, turning occasionally. Cover and refrigerate remaining marinade.

Drain and discard marinade from turkey. Sprinkle turkey with pepper and 1/2 teaspoon salt. In a large nonstick skillet, cook turkey in remaining oil for 10-12 minutes or until no longer pink, turning once. Remove and keep warm.

Combine cornstarch, broth, reserved marinade and remaining salt until smooth; add to skillet. Bring to a boil; cook and stir for 1-2 minutes or until thickened. Slice turkey; serve with sauce. **Yield:** 6 servings.

Editor's Note: If using apple juice in place of wine, add 3 tablespoons cider vinegar to the marinade.

Turkey Ravioli Lasagna

(Pictured at right)

Anne Plesmid, Sagamore Hills, Ohio

I came up with this "shortcut" lasagna one day when the dinner hour was fast approaching and all I had in the freezer was some frozen ravioli. Now I make it often, and my husband and son devour it.

1 pound ground turkey
1/2 teaspoon garlic powder
Salt and pepper to taste
1 cup grated carrots
1 cup sliced fresh mushrooms
1 tablespoon olive oil
1 jar (28 ounces) spaghetti sauce
1 package (25 ounces) frozen cheese ravioli, cooked and drained
3 cups (12 ounces) shredded mozzarella cheese
1/2 cup grated Parmesan cheese
Minced fresh parsley, optional

In a skillet, cook turkey over medium heat until no longer pink; drain. Sprinkle with garlic powder, salt and pepper; set aside.

In a saucepan, cook carrots and mushrooms in oil until tender. Stir in the spaghetti sauce. Spread 1/2 cup sauce in a greased 13-in. x 9-in. x 2-in. baking dish. Layer with half of the ravioli, spaghetti sauce mixture, turkey and cheeses. Repeat layers. Sprinkle with parsley if desired.

Cover and bake at 375° for 25-30 minutes or until bubbly. Uncover; bake 10 minutes longer. Let stand 15 minutes before serving. **Yield:** 12 servings.

Garden Turkey Burgers

Sandy Kitzmiller, Unityville, Pennsylvania

These moist burgers get plenty of color and flavor from onion, zucchini and red pepper. I often make the mixture ahead of time and put it in the refrigerator. Later, I can put the burgers on the grill while whipping up a salad or side dish.

1 cup old-fashioned oats
3/4 cup chopped onion
3/4 cup finely chopped sweet red *or* green pepper
1/2 cup shredded zucchini
1/4 cup ketchup
2 garlic cloves, minced
1/4 teaspoon salt
1 pound ground turkey
6 whole wheat hamburger buns, split and toasted

Coat grill rack with nonstick cooking spray before starting the grill. In a bowl, combine oats, onion, red pepper, zucchini, ketchup, garlic and salt. Add turkey and mix well. Shape into six 1/2-in.-thick patties.

Grill, covered, over indirect medium heat for 6 minutes on each side or until a meat thermometer reads 165°. Serve on buns. **Yield:** 6 burgers.

edges. Brush pastry with cream.

Bake at 400° for 25-30 minutes or until golden brown. If necessary, cover the edges of the crust with foil to prevent overbrowning. **Yield:** 6 servings.

Turkey Scallopini

(Pictured below)

Karen Adams, Seymour, Indiana

Quick-cooking turkey breast slices make this recipe a winner when you only have a few minutes to fix a satisfying meal. I've also used flattened boneless skinless chicken breast halves in place of the turkey for this entree.

> 6 turkey breast slices (about 1-1/2 pounds)
> 1/4 cup all-purpose flour
> 1/8 teaspoon salt
> 1/8 teaspoon pepper
> 1 egg
> 2 tablespoons water
> 1 cup soft bread crumbs
> 1/2 cup grated Parmesan cheese
> 1/4 cup butter
> Minced fresh parsley

Pound turkey to 1/4-in. thickness. In a shallow bowl, combine flour, salt and pepper. In another bowl, beat egg and water. On a plate, combine the bread crumbs

Turkey Potpie

(Pictured above)

Cheryl Arnold, Lake Zurich, Illinois

Family and guests rave about this hearty potpie and its light flaky crust. The "secret" crust ingredients are Parmesan cheese and instant mashed potato flakes. On busy days, I prepare this in the morning and just bake it at night.

> 1 can (10-3/4 ounces) condensed cream of mushroom soup, undiluted
> 1 can (5 ounces) evaporated milk
> 1/4 cup minced fresh parsley *or* 1 tablespoon dried parsley flakes
> 1/2 teaspoon dried thyme
> 3 cups cubed cooked turkey
> 1 package (10 ounces) frozen mixed vegetables, thawed
> 1/4 teaspoon salt
> 1/4 teaspoon pepper
> CRUST:
> 3/4 cup instant mashed potato flakes
> 3/4 cup all-purpose flour
> 1/4 cup grated Parmesan cheese
> 1/3 cup butter
> 1/4 cup ice water
> Half-and-half cream

In a bowl, combine the first four ingredients. Stir in turkey, vegetables, salt and pepper. Spoon into a greased 11-in. x 7-in. x 2-in. baking dish.

For crust, combine potato flakes, flour and Parmesan in a bowl; cut in butter until crumbly. Add water, 1 tablespoon at a time, tossing lightly with a fork until the dough forms a ball. On a lightly floured surface, roll the dough to fit baking dish. Cut vents in crust, using a small tree or star cutter if desired. Place over filling; flute

Drain pineapple, reserving 1/4 cup juice (discard remaining juice or save for another use). In a bowl, combine the reserved pineapple juice, brown sugar, oil, Worcestershire sauce, garlic and mustard; mix well. Pour 1/3 cup into a large resealable plastic bag; add the turkey. Seal bag and turn to coat; refrigerate for 2-3 hours. Cover and refrigerate remaining marinade.

If grilling the kabobs, coat grill rack with nonstick cooking spray before starting the grill. Drain and discard marinade from turkey.

On eight metal or soaked wooden skewers, alternately thread vegetables, turkey and pineapple. Grill, uncovered, over medium heat or broil 4-6 in. from the heat for 4-5 minutes on each side or until meat is no longer pink, turning three times and basting frequently with reserved marinade. **Yield:** 4 servings.

and Parmesan cheese. Dredge turkey in flour mixture, then dip in egg mixture and coat with crumbs. Melt butter in a skillet over medium-high heat; cook turkey for 2-3 minutes on each side or until meat juices run clear and coating is golden brown. Sprinkle with parsley. **Yield:** 6 servings.

Turkey Pepper Kabobs

(Pictured above)

Traci Goodman, Paducah, Kentucky

This is a summertime favorite at our house. The turkey is a nice change of pace and goes great with the sweet basting sauce and pineapple.

    1 can (8 ounces) unsweetened pineapple
      chunks
  1/4 cup packed brown sugar
    2 tablespoons canola oil
    2 tablespoons Worcestershire sauce
    1 garlic clove, minced
    1 teaspoon prepared mustard
    1 pound turkey tenderloin, cut into 1-inch
      cubes
    1 large sweet onion, cut into 3/4-inch pieces
    1 large green pepper, cut into 1-inch pieces
    1 large sweet red pepper, cut into 1-inch
      pieces

Turkey with Cherry Stuffing

Virginia Sacchetta, Leesburg, Florida

This moist stuffing, with its fruity blend of raisins and tart cherries, is a sweet twist on a traditional version. It's a tasty complement to tender poultry slices. Be prepared to dish up second helpings when you serve this bird.

  3/4 cup chopped celery
  1/3 cup chopped onion
    2 tablespoons butter
  3/4 teaspoon dried thyme
  1/4 teaspoon poultry seasoning
    5 cups seasoned stuffing cubes
  3/4 cup golden raisins
  3/4 cup chicken broth
    1 can (14-1/2 ounces) pitted tart cherries,
      drained
    1 turkey (10 to 12 pounds)
    2 tablespoons vegetable oil

In a saucepan, saute celery and onion in butter until tender. Stir in thyme and poultry seasoning. In a large bowl, combine stuffing, raisins and celery mixture. Add broth and cherries; toss to mix.

Loosely stuff turkey just before baking. Skewer openings; tie drumsticks together. Place the turkey, breast side up, on a rack in a roasting pan. Brush with oil.

Bake, uncovered, at 325° for 4 to 4-1/2 hours or until a meat thermometer reads 180° for turkey and 165° for stuffing. Baste occasionally with pan drippings. Cover loosely with foil if turkey browns too quickly.

Cover and let stand for 20 minutes before removing the stuffing and carving the turkey. If desired, thicken pan drippings for gravy. **Yield:** 10-12 servings (6 cups stuffing).

Editor's Note: The stuffing may be prepared as directed and baked separately in a greased 2-qt. baking dish. Cover and bake at 325° for 50-60 minutes. Uncover and bake the turkey 10 minutes longer or until lightly browned.

General Index of Recipes & Tips

Recipes are listed by ingredient. The Chicken category is organized by type, cooking method and/or food category.

✓ Recipe includes Nutritional Analysis and Diabetic Exchanges

✓ Recipe includes Nutritional Analysis and Diabetic Exchanges

Alphabetical Listing